Unlock Team Brilliance with Synergy Boosting Techniques

Jacqueline .R Cassidy

Funny helpful tips:

Life's melody is sweetest when sung with passion and authenticity.

Stay committed to open dialogue; it prevents misunderstandings.

Unlock Team Brilliance with Synergy Boosting Techniques : Maximize Your Team's Potential with Effective Synergy Techniques for Enhanced Brilliance.

Life advices:

Stay updated with technology; it's an ever-evolving tool that can enhance efficiency.

Stay authentic; your unique essence is your strength.

Introduction

This is a comprehensive resource that explores the power of alignment in the context of business and leadership. It begins by defining leadership and highlighting the importance of alignment, which includes having a clear vision, inspiring commitment, and taking aligned action.

The book introduces key principles of alignment, such as the iterative co-creation principle, the SHUVA principle (Seen, Heard, Understood, Valued, Appreciated), and the versatility principle. These principles provide a foundation for understanding and implementing alignment strategies.

Readers are guided through the steps and 5 Cs of alignment, including preparing proposals, conducting brainstorming sessions, running online surveys, hosting focus groups, and presenting proposals effectively. Testing for commitment and techniques like Fist to Five polling are also discussed.

Preparing for alignment meetings is crucial, and the book covers initial considerations, defining where to start, determining levels of agreement, setting quorums, and defining constraints. Stakeholder mapping and deciding who to include are important aspects of this process.

The book provides insights into running alignment meetings efficiently, covering logistics, meeting roles (leader, facilitator, scribe, timekeeper), and issuing invitations. It emphasizes the importance of ground rules, such as balancing participation, fostering open communication, and honoring confidentiality.

Alignment is explored from different angles, including top-down alignment, bottom-up alignment, and sideways alignment. Each approach is accompanied by valuable tips and strategies for effective implementation.

Inevitably, challenges may arise during the alignment process, and the book offers troubleshooting advice. It addresses disruptive behaviors and provides guidance on how to handle them, including coaching and managing difficult behaviors. The book also encourages self-reflection and suggests that leaders consider their own impact on alignment.

In summary, this book is a practical guide that equips leaders with the knowledge and tools needed to foster alignment within their organizations. It emphasizes the importance of inclusive leadership and provides actionable steps to create a culture of alignment, collaboration, and commitment.

Contents

SECTION 1

THE POWER OF ALIGNMENT

CHAPTER 1

ALIGNMENT AND BUSINESS

Alignment: noun

> Arrangement in a straight line, or in correct or appropriate relative positions; position of agreement or alliance

Last winter, on my way to Denver, I hit a pothole and knocked my wheels out of alignment. Suddenly, I had to drive the car with a tight grip on the steering wheel to keep from veering around like a drunk driver. Rather than get it taken care of right away, I just kept driving with my wheels out of alignment. Not only were my tires wearing unevenly, I stupidly ran the risk of a blowout. By the time I made it to the auto shop, I needed two new tires.

With my new wheels aligned, I was blown away. I could just cruise down the highway with one finger on the steering wheel. If it wasn't dangerous, I probably could have driven hands-free for a few hundred miles while reading a newspaper. Alignment made that possible.

Turning ideas into realities is a lot like driving a car. The key players involved need to be in the appropriate positions; otherwise, things will drag.

As a business coach, one of the first questions I ask my clients is, "What do you want to achieve?" Here are a few examples of what I have heard:

- "I want to build a software platform that will transform how people work."
- "I want my team to work more collaboratively across silos."
- "I want our decisions to be driven by data."
- "I want all employees to embrace safety as a priority."

It's wonderful if you are blessed with great ideas and vision. However, even the best ideas are worthless if you can't get any traction behind them. In business, you have to get work done through others, and it can be quite a challenge. To do it well, you need to get your team members on the same page so they can deliver on goals when you aren't around. If you don't do this effectively, they will either flounder or feel micromanaged.

While aligning direct reports is hard enough, at least you have some jurisdiction over them. It's much harder to align someone you don't have authority over, such as the boss, upper management, peers, vendors, and clients. Even CEOs have board members and investors they have to line up.

Alignment becomes harder in a business that has been around awhile because people become entrenched in the "way things are done around here." If this is your reality, don't give up. All organizations must evolve. Someone has to challenge the status quo; otherwise, the business risks being killed off by agile competitors and disruptive technology.

Alignment is especially challenging in a sizeable, multilayered organization where functions are specialized. Divisions and departments often become siloed. When something is improved in one department, it can have a negative consequence in another. Larger organizations especially need systems thinkers who connect the parts of the system and get it working as a cohesive whole.

All businesses require alignment because groups of all kinds, including leadership teams, boards, employees, customers, vendors, and investors achieve more when aligned. Alignment isn't just about getting groups to agree. It's required whenever any two people come together to make a plan, whether they're business partners, a boss and direct report, a consultant and client, or two colleagues working together. Imagine how much you could accomplish with alignment between all these parties.

Alignment drives growth and scalability in business. To scale and grow, you have to get others to do things, and they, in turn, have to get others to do things, and so on. When your employees are aligned, they run on their own steam and don't need your will to move them along. Furthermore, when customers are inspired and committed to your mission, products, and services, they become passionate advocates for your business's success.

When it comes to business, there are infinite areas that require alignment. I like to say that alignment is useful to address the Ps and Qs of business. The Ps are purpose, people, pay, policies, processes, platforms, plans, and profitability. Then there are the Qs. The Qs are the big questions like: What is our mission, vision, and values? What company culture should we strive for? How can we stand out from the competition? There is no shortage of important topics on which to align.

If this feels overwhelming, here is a quick MSF to make it simple. In business, create alignment on these three levers, and you will build a culture of high performance:

The Three Levers of Organizational Alignment

1. Set direction—agree on the mission, vision, values, strategy, and goals of the organization or team
2. Create the clock—agree on systems, processes, and the cadence for individuals and groups to coordinate their work
3. Empower people—agree on roles and responsibilities and how to create a workplace culture where everyone can thrive

Now let's take a second to think about the cost of *mis*alignment. How many dollars are wasted in redundant work, ideas that fail to launch, decisions reversed, and policies not followed? We may never know. You don't have to be a financial genius to figure out that the cost of misalignment is astronomical.

Let's take one of the most obvious downsides of misalignment: time wasted in meetings where nothing gets decided. For example, if you have a management team with five people at an annual salary of $100,000 per person and they spend an average of fifteen hours a week in meetings, the team's weekly meeting cost is $4,076, and the annual costs are a shocking $212,000! If the team could reduce the time wasted in meetings by 40 percent, they would save $85,000 per year! While the savings is easy to calculate, the real value is the growth that happens when good ideas finally land new customers and lead to profits.

I hope by now, I've made my case. Alignment is flat-out good for business. It still may seem like there is never enough time to get everyone on the same page. But in business, you can't afford not to.

CHAPTER 2

ALIGNMENT AND LEADERSHIP

"If you want to go fast, go alone. If you want to go far, go together."
—AFRICAN PROVERB

Over a decade ago, we helped a leadership team formulate their three-year strategic plan using alignment practices. The team, which had been chronically overcommitted, finally agreed on the common goals they were all jazzed about. The leaders left fired-up and focused. Within a short time, the business unit's performance moved from the bottom quartile to the top. I recently ran into one of the team members, Aidan, and asked her what had since transpired. Aidan shared that those who continued leading inclusively using alignment skills "are now running almost everything in the company."

I have since come to realize that fostering alignment is THE critical skill that separates dreamers from leaders who get things done. To reinforce this idea, I'd like to back up for a minute and clarify how leadership and alignment are linked.

DEFINITION OF LEADERSHIP

LEADERSHIP IS...

...the art
and science...

...of inspiring
committed...

...and aligned
action...

...towards a
clear vision.

ART AND SCIENCE

Great leadership is an art because everyone practices it differently. One leader may be quiet and introverted and do a lot of writing. Another may be charismatic, outgoing, and hard-charging. Yet another may operate silently, encouraging others behind the scenes. Leadership is also a science. You can actually get a PhD in leadership these days, which didn't exist when I started working in the field back in the nineties. There is a lot of solid research and evidence regarding what it takes to be a good leader and how we can reproduce those variables. Yes, some are born leaders, but most can improve by following inclusive practices proven to foster followership.

VISION

"The very essence of leadership is that you have to have a vision."
THEODORE HESBURGH

The most essential component of leadership is vision. Without a vision of a future better than the past, there is no leadership. Instead, you have the status quo—or worse, devolution. There are many examples of visionary leaders, like Joy Mangano, the Miracle Mop inventor; Elon Musk, the founder of SpaceX and co-founder of Tesla; and others like Ray Kroc, a pioneer of the fast-food industry who created a whole new way to serve the customer.

These humans are blessed with extraordinary gifts to envision new solutions to old problems. Some visionaries seem to be clairvoyant; they can visualize a future no one else has thought of yet. If you don't have visionary superpowers, don't worry. Your vision doesn't have to be unique to inspire followers. You can move someone else's vision forward or craft a vision with the talented people around you. Regardless, your ability to clarify a vision into a worthy pursuit is fundamental to your role as a leader.

INSPIRING COMMITMENT

"A leader has the vision and conviction that a dream can be achieved. He inspires the power and energy to get it done."

RALPH LAUREN

As an individual, you can do many things on your own, but if you really want to lead, you have to get others to do things of their own free will. Too often, workers do things out of compliance, not commitment. When this is the case, we use a lot of carrots and sticks to keep them on track. While rewards and punishments are useful to get work done, without the employee's commitment, things fall apart the minute we turn our backs. Good leaders know that commitment trumps compliance every time and is key to an engaged work culture.

ALIGNED ACTION

"A genuine leader is not a searcher for consensus but a molder of consensus."

MARTIN LUTHER KING, JR.

Now we finally come to the link between leadership and alignment. Alignment occurs when two or more people come together to make an agreement that ignites action. Often, you can get your team inspired and committed, but they lack alignment. When your staff pulls in multiple directions, they lose momentum. Staying on track requires constant vigilance. With alignment, silos break down, your team works together, and things move forward. While inspirational leaders can get folks jazzed-up about things, those who foster aligned action get traction and momentum behind great ideas.

In summary, you can't lead without alignment. The bottom line is this: if you really want to lead, you just have to get good at aligning people.

SECTION 1. MEMORABLE SUCCESS FORMULAS

- Three Levers of Organizational Alignment: set direction, create the clock, empower people.
- Fostering alignment is THE critical skill that separates dreamers from leaders.
- Leadership is the art and science of inspiring committed and aligned action toward a clear vision.
- Commitment trumps compliance every time.

SECTION 2

THE 3 PRINCIPLES OF ALIGNMENT

"Success is a science; if you have the conditions, you get the result."
—OSCAR WILOE

To this day, the principles my parents taught me guide my daily steps. For example, when I was a kid, my dad, Willson, took jobs that brought us from Venezuela to Louisiana to Alabama to Mexico to Argentina. My mom, Maryanne, was a trooper; each move required packing up six kids' belongings and rebuilding a home in a new and often strange place. The first thing she always unpacked was a little plaque that read, "bloom where you are planted," which she placed ceremoniously in the kitchen window.

For our family, "bloom where you are planted" was not just a platitude; it was a guiding principle. Wherever we lived, we learned the language and made lifelong friends. Mom loved to cook local recipes. In Venezuela, we ate hallacas wrapped in banana leaves; in Louisiana, we sucked sugar cane; in Alabama, we ate shrimp and grits; in Mexico, flan casero; and in Argentina, empanadas criollas. If we ever whined about what we left behind, we were reminded of the blessings and possibilities of our new home. This guiding principle still serves me to this day. Whenever change knocks on my door, I remind myself to bloom. This is the power of a principle: no matter what changes, the principle remains the same, providing a compass so you can find your path forward.

The three principles in this section are your compass for alignment and the foundation for all the practices in this book.

The three principles of alignment are:

The Iterative Co-creation Principle

The SHUVA Principle

The Versatility Principle

CHAPTER 3

THE ITERATIVE CO-CREATION PRINCIPLE

Most ideas are not born great; they are made great through many conversations. *No matter how great your idea is, you can always improve it by consulting others.* Multiple studies prove that on average, large groups come up with better solutions than small groups or any one person.

A great example comes from the book *The Wisdom of Crowds* by James Surowiecki. The book recounts the story of a London exhibition where participants placed wagers on the weight of an ox. It turned out that the average of almost 800 guesses was closer to the weight of the ox than any one person's estimate, including the butcher who was supposed to be an expert. The average guess was 1,197 pounds; the ox's actual weight was 1,198 pounds. Pretty amazing, right? What this story illustrates is the simple truth that groups are often smarter than the smartest individual within the group.

By consulting as many people as you can to help shape your ideas, you create a brain trust. By including people from different parts of the system, you gain many perspectives on the problem like facets of a prism. When a decision is informed by those it impacts, it is more likely to be sound and well-received.

Here is yet another reason to not only consult others but to invite them to co-create with you: ownership. *People don't take down what they build*, so including stakeholders in shaping solutions avoids the future destruction of your most recent resolution. The more people included in decisions before they are finalized, the more traction you get, and the more likely you are to ditch bad ideas before they fail.

By including others in formulating realistic plans that they are fired-up about, you not only avoid pitfalls, *you also create teams on fire that never burn out*. While it may take longer to involve others on the front end, the payoff is big on the back end. There is no need to "hold them accountable." Instead, those involved in formulating plans hold themselves accountable.

I learned this lesson many years ago when I worked as chief of staff for a senior vice president, Thom, at Amoco, a major energy company. Back before cloud-based teaming tools were a thing, Thom had asked me to work with IT to create an intranet to help everyone understand what their coworkers were up to and collaborate online. I did a few interviews to find out what his staff wanted and worked with IT to build an intranet system that would fit the bill. I then presented the solution to his team of forty technologists in an elaborate launch. The launch included a presentation, a Q&A, a video, and even a scavenger hunt to get everyone excited about the new platform. It started with a bang, but within a month of launch, NOT ONE person was using the intranet we had invested so much time and money into building. It felt like a colossal failure, and I wasn't sure whether to blame myself, the technology, or the lame employees that never seemed to follow through.

Around that time, I was reading Peter Block's book *Flawless Consulting: A Guide to Getting Your Expertise Used.* Block's book helped me see that I was not working collaboratively enough with my clients for them to own the solution. Instead, by trying to be efficient and build a brilliant solution for the staff, I had set us all up for failure.

So, I swallowed my pride and suggested we start all over again—from scratch. I asked Thom to sponsor a cross-departmental team to come up with a better intranet solution. The group convened six times over three months, designing the new system from scratch. When the new system launched, it was virtually the same as the one launched six months before, but with one huge difference: everyone used it. This experience has stuck with me and informs how I approach working with others to achieve anything. I have seen firsthand how iterative co-creation fosters relationships and exponentially expands the reach and impact of solutions created. Was creating the intranet twice efficient? No, but it paid off in that the solution was functional and widely adopted.

When you work co-creatively with others, you need to be patient and know that the path to alignment is not always short or straight. Not everyone moves at the same speed, and people are seldom in the same place. Now that more companies are global, it is not unusual for teams to span many time zones. These days, the complexity of problems and the sheer number of stakeholders involved make it impractical to get all players convened at once.

Even if you come to a decision-making process prepared, as deliberation occurs, new information emerges, missing data is discovered, and absent players need to be looped in. While this may drive you crazy, you are better served to accept the reality that alignment is iterative. There is, however, a bright side to that. *When it comes to innovation, iteration is your friend*. Often when you first bring up an idea, people will reject it. This is to be expected; in fact, a person may need to hear something seven times before they hear it the first time. For this reason, iteration is your friend, allowing for nuances to be fully understood before a final decision is made. By breaking the decision-making process into multiple steps, you give people time to warm up to an idea.

Keep in mind: *Creativity is crushed when rushed*. I can't tell you how often I am asked to facilitate a decision that takes twenty minutes to explain in a thirty-minute time slot. Ten minutes isn't enough time for someone to process a twenty-minute proposal, much less offer helpful feedback. Creativity requires "noodle and soak time." Many poor decisions are made when groups are not provided enough time to deliberate. When it comes to big ideas, *efficiency is just too small a god to serve*! Time must be invested.

This is where the beauty of iteration comes in. Rather than plan to present an idea and reach agreement in one fell swoop, break things down into multiple steps, knowing that the path to alignment is more of a marathon than a sprint. Rather than pressuring people to make decisions on the spot, plan to convene multiple times. Build in "soak time" between each session. Each time, be sure to knit things together by reorienting players to what has happened since they last met. By following the principle of iterative co-creation with intention, you provide the space and time for healthy deliberation and allow creativity to bubble up.

For more tips on how to plan time for alignment sessions, see chapter 12.

CHAPTER 4

THE SHUVA PRINCIPLE

When we come together in a group to get aligned, it may appear that we are all here to solve the problem at hand. While that is true, under that truth is a more profound one: we are all here to become well-regarded members of the group. However, unless all the members of the group also want that for each other, the environment is not safe for interpersonal risk-taking and playing full out.

Google conducted an extensive two-year study on team performance called Project Aristotle. As Charles Duhigg wrote in the *The New York Times* in 2016, the study revealed that the highest-performing teams have one thing in common: the belief that team members won't be punished when they make a mistake or speak up. This is called psychological safety, and studies show that it allows for moderate risk-taking, speaking your mind, creativity, and sticking your neck out without fear of having it cut off.

Psychological safety can be hard to come by, especially in a company environment where our job, reputation, and income is at stake. While you may not realize it, we have instincts that protect us from danger, and our brain can process a provocation by a boss, competitive coworker, or dismissive subordinate as a life-or-death threat. Our amygdala, the alarm bell in the brain, ignites the fight-or-flight response, hijacking our logical thinking and shutting down perspective and analytical reasoning. Quite literally, just when we need them most, we lose our minds. While that fight-or-flight reaction may save us in life-or-death situations, it handicaps our ability to work together and speak our minds. This might seem overly dramatic, but you must be aware this is happening so you can guide everyone into the safety zone by creating an environment of trust, curiosity, and positive regard for one another. In such an environment, we all become more open to possibilities.

Jennifer Joyce, my former business partner and co-creator of the 4 Steps and 5 Cs of Alignment, created what she calls the Golden Rule of Psychological Safety:

"We must find a solution for you AND for me. If one of us is left unhappy, the relationship/trust will suffer. In addition, the issue will be left unresolved on one side or the other."

The one thing you can do to create psychological safety is to always offer SHUVA to everyone. SHUVA is an acronym I created to describe a basic need universal to all humans: the need to be **S**een, **H**eard, **U**nderstood, **V**alued, and **A**ppreciated.

Think about it. When you feel seen, heard, understood, valued, and appreciated, it feels terrific. You can be yourself and express yourself. SHUVA is the path to true alignment because all ideas, including doubts and reservations, are welcome. When I feel SHUVA from a person or group, I am more willing to expend the extra energy required to hash out areas of misalignment. Keep in mind: you don't have to agree with what somebody says to offer them SHUVA.

If you do nothing else in this book but provide as much SHUVA as possible to everyone on your path, you will go far in creating alignment. While it may seem obvious what it means to see, hear, understand, value, and appreciate, below are a few nuances of how to SHUVA well.

SEEN

Everyone is moving so fast, they seldom take the time to see the people around them. Many people feel invisible and isolated. When you give your time and attention to someone, they feel seen. Start by being thoughtful about whom you include in your co-creative process. When you invite someone to co-create with you, share why their involvement matters to the project and to you personally.

Use eye contact. Eye contact is key, but you would be surprised how seldom it happens. When my children were young, I taught them to always acknowledge parents who had hosted them before leaving a play date. My son was shy and often struggled with this task. I would ask him, “Did you thank Ms. Annie before you left?” If he said yes, I would ask, “Great, what color are Ms. Annie’s eyes?” If he didn’t know, I’d ask him to go back in and find out.

Today when coaching leaders, I ask them to make a list of their employees and others they co-create with and to make sure they know the color of their eyes. While you are looking at someone’s eyes, be sure to notice their gifts, talents, and personal struggles.

HEARD

Hearing requires time, so plan accordingly. When working in a group, track who has spoken, and make sure everyone has the chance to comment. Don’t interrupt, just let the speaker talk and focus on what they are saying, intending to catch every word.

Good listening will not only improve your understanding; it will improve the quality of what is shared. Have you ever noticed that a band plays better music when a crowd is listening? People are like that too. We often think the sender shapes the receiver, but in reality, the receiver also shapes the sender. This is especially true for external processors who discover what they are thinking by talking out loud. You would be amazed at what even one minute of quality listening can do to accelerate the path to alignment.

UNDERSTOOD

Understanding requires listening with an open mind until all points have been expressed and clarified. If you feel confused while someone is speaking, you aren't there yet. It is crucial to keep listening until you feel clear. That said, understanding is a two-way street. Not only must the receiver listen enough to "get" what the sender meant, the sender also has to feel that the receiver "got" the message intended. Even if you think you "got" it, take a few minutes to voice your understanding and confirm that it matches the intended message.

To understand, you have to move from a literal point of view to a figurative one. Understanding requires listening **under** the words shared for what has meaning and heart for the sender. When you mirror back to the person what you heard in your own words, be sure to include a few things you've read between the lines so that the sender feels heard on a deeper level.

Once when I was facilitating an alignment session, one upset participant complained that a colleague had gotten fired for noncompliance with an unfair policy. In fact, the person had been fired for other reasons. Instead of correcting the misperception, I listened to uncover why she felt the policy was unfair. Before long, she was able to get out some key points that helped us reshape the policy.

The key is to listen for feelings that haven't been expressed yet. Listen for what really matters to the person speaking. Get used to the idea that people might be incorrect with facts and figures while still having a valid overall point. Listen for the point to emerge. Listening to understand is more than a cognitive experience; when something registers as understood, both parties feel it in their heads, hearts, and guts.

VALUED

My former boss, Geri, was quite strong-willed and confident. She often made an effort to run ideas by us so we would feel included. However, she was only humoring us, and we could tell. In reality, she made things worse by asking for our ideas and then just railroading us onto the path she came in with.

In contrast, another former boss, Doug, was genuinely interested in what all team members felt. Working for Doug was a highlight of my career. He often held impromptu meetings where ideas were generated and opinions shared. It wasn't unusual for these conversations to take place over a few beers at the nearby hangout. As a result, we became a rock star team, eager to tackle any task he threw at us.

I have stayed friends with Doug and have been amazed at how he can recount conversations from over twenty years ago and how they shaped his thinking. It meant a lot to me then, and it means even more to me now.

You value someone when you "listen to learn" with the intent to be changed. Listening to learn is powered by curiosity and the belief that what others share may very well change your life or unveil something you never considered. This is in sharp contrast to ordinary listening. Ordinarily, we listen for what we agree or disagree with, often only paying attention to the commentary in our heads.

We all like to think that we are open-minded, but the fact is we often aren't even aware that we have arrived at the table with a closed mind. Listening to learn entails vulnerability and a willingness to be surprised. Let go of assumptions, and take in ambiguity. You don't have to agree with a person to value them; you just have to give their ideas a shot. When you disagree with the sender's point of view, assume there is a reason they think the way they do. Before abandoning any idea, ask yourself, what am I missing?

APPRECIATED

Appreciation is the act of expressing gratitude for what others bring forward, and it is the icing on the SHUVA cake. The simple act of saying thank you is often enough, but it never hurts to double down on appreciation with a small gift or personal note. Doug was a leader who nailed the skill of meaningful appreciation. When Doug started his own company, he wanted to find a creative way to let his employees know how much he personally admired their efforts.

Every year, Doug got a stack of crisp new one-hundred-dollar bills from the bank to hand out whenever one of his employees went the extra mile. Doug's bills became so prized that employees often framed and displayed them on their walls. While you may not be in a position to pass out cash, it is not that hard to keep a stack of thank you cards on hand to personally express your feelings of gratitude. Small, thoughtful gestures like cards, flowers, coffee mugs, hats, or tickets to events also make recipients feel treasured.

Public acknowledgment is also very important. Periodically take a minute to thank participants in a meeting or by email. When someone works with you who is not in your department, be sure to CC their boss on any letters of thanks.

Now that you have learned about SHUVA, you are probably thinking, “SHUVA does feel good. I want some too!” To get SHUVA to come your way, it helps to be proactive. Teach others what SHUVA is and ask for it. SHUVA can become a part of your team’s lingo. On our team, we often say: “I’ve got an idea to share and need a little SHUVA.” This signal reminds us to slow down and sweeten the quality of our attention. We have also taken to closing conversations by saying, “I SHUVA you!” to express appreciation for ideas shared. Since implementing the SHUVA principle in our team’s daily interactions, alignment has been much easier to achieve.

CHAPTER 5

THE VERSATILITY PRINCIPLE

Most modern businesses started in an era when men were the primary breadwinners and creators of industries. Because of these origins, many companies operate in a patriarchal fashion rooted in the masculine principle. A fundamental belief that shapes the masculine principle is that to survive, one must be independent and compete to win. The masculine principle reinforces the idea that great leaders are competitive, confident, frank, courageous, objective, and out front. An adage that represents the masculine principle is "when in charge, be in charge."

For many years, both men and women in organizations held a subconscious belief that these masculine qualities were synonymous with leadership, while feminine qualities such as being nurturing and accommodating were antithetical to leadership and sound business. After World War II, thanks to reliable contraception, women entered the workforce in droves. Eventually, gender-mixing at work and the rise of feminism reshaped how both men and women viewed the task of leading. Over time, an alternative view of leadership shaped by the feminine principle emerged. The feminine principle is based on the belief that because humans are interdependent, collaboration, not competition, is the key to survival. The feminine principle reinforces the idea that great leaders are collaborative, diplomatic, careful, emotionally sensitive, and humble servants of others. A motto of leaders that follows the feminine principle is “true leaders don’t create followers, they create more leaders.”

The interesting thing to point out here is that the masculine and feminine principles hold **equally valid** yet completely **opposing** views of what it takes to survive, thrive, and lead effectively.

THE MASCULINE PRINCIPLE	THE FEMININE PRINCIPLE
Be Independent	Be Interdependent
Compete	Collaborate
Be Objective	Be Emotionally Sensitive
Be Confident	Be Humble
Be Bold	Be Careful
Push Ideas Forward	Pull Ideas from Others
Be Firm	Be Flexible
Be Tough	Be Tender
Inspire	Encourage

Because the masculine and feminine principles are polar opposite belief systems, most people lead with *either* the masculine *or* the feminine principle operating subconsciously in the background. While the masculine and the feminine principles are equally beneficial to leadership, both principles also have many downsides when it comes to reaching alignment.

Those who follow the masculine principle see the work of alignment as a top-down *telling and selling* proposition. Someone in charge has the vision and makes decisions. They then cascade action plans downward using command and control tactics. While this form of leadership works, often those being led from the masculine principle feel *forced* to comply with directives. Even when people agree with the directives, they fall off track because they may not understand *why* they need to follow them or how they tie to larger goals.

The downside of masculine leadership is that the followers own less of the solution. There is less accountability because being told what to do puts the brain into passive mode. To fully engage others to be more proactive, you must involve the emotive and sensory parts of the brain in decision-making.

My client Erica, an electrical engineer, worked in a male-dominated field in which the masculine principle was the norm. Erica believed she had to be forceful in pursuing her agenda. She often was the first to speak up and could become stubborn when anyone challenged her assertions. At times, she would work to "get buy-in" from others using logic and convincing arguments to remove objections. Unfortunately, this attempt to include others fell short because it was just a thinly veiled attempt to win using too much masculine "push energy."

Men and women who lead from the masculine principle value objectivity and therefore follow an unspoken rule to avoid talking about feelings. While being objective has many merits, leading without sensitivity to emotions seldom works. As long as you are dealing with humans, you proceed at your peril if you don't factor feelings into the conversation. Decisions made objectively just come from the head and minimize the wisdom of the heart and gut. Even if the decision makes logical sense, you pay big time when feelings are suppressed, and you lose the passion that comes when the head, heart, and gut are lined up.

The masculine principle is exemplified by a bold, visionary, courageous hero who wins by compellingly pitching their idea. Once the concept is adopted, the hero gains recognition for being a "rock star." In real life, wowing others is not leading. You may be brilliant in coming up with good ideas, but you are operating as an individual contributor rather than a leader who engages others' gifts and talents.

Those who lead using the masculine principle believe:

- Power comes from the top
- Efficiency is key
- There is only one right answer (mine)
- Facts and logic trump feelings
- If people end up dissatisfied, "Oh well, they can just go elsewhere."

You know you are operating from the masculine principle when agendas are tight and the focus is on getting stuff done. At times, this can be good, but in general, the masculine principle overvalues the task at hand and undervalues the importance of relationships. Leaders who follow the masculine principle do a poor job of empowering others to think bigger and more thoroughly and to grow.

The primary alternative to leading with the masculine principle is leading with the feminine principle. The feminine principle is based on the belief that since we are interdependent, no one should be more powerful than another and power should always be shared. The feminine principle encourages leaders to be much less visible, withhold their opinions, and use "pull energy" to draw solutions from the group. When following the feminine principle, leaders focus on asking questions to engage and encourage others. Feelings and intuition are prized, as there is no alignment until all are satisfied.

My client Perry, a field tech manager, subconsciously led with the feminine principle. Field techs were hard to come by, so Perry wanted to keep his staff "fat and happy." The field techs needed more consistency across shifts, but they never seemed to be able to agree on anything. Many of Perry's field techs were dismissive of management and viewed them as "pointy-haired bosses from *Dilbert*." Rather than stepping up and getting the team to commit to a plan, Perry resorted to letting everyone do things their own way. And, he was usually left to clean up the mess afterward.

Those who follow the feminine principle elevate another version of a mythic hero, a humble servant with no need for recognition or ownership of ideas. While this approach is noble, it often makes it impossible to get everyone in a room aligned, as too many ideas are deliberated at once. When final decisions must equally please all stakeholders, decisions are diluted to the lowest common denominator. The belief that power distribution should always be equal can make one hesitant to step up and lead when challenges arise for fear they might be perceived as domineering.

Groups that operate from the feminine principle may never reach agreement. Lacking focus and a clear leader, meetings run over, and nothing gets decided. To avoid triggering conflict in these situations, people *fake* agreement. They often say yes to things, but never say when things will get done. Or they pretend to be happy to avoid conflict. You can always tell if a leader or group is overdoing the feminine principle when you feel that something is off, but no one ever talks about it. Instead, they tiptoe around the elephant in the room.

Those who lead using the feminine principle believe:

- Power should be equally shared
- Flexibility is key

- There are many solutions
- Feelings must be satisfied
- If the task takes a long time, "Oh well, we need to make everyone happy."

You will know you are operating with an *overly* feminine approach if the agenda is too loose, and the focus is all on people and processes, not on completing the task at hand.

To help clients like Erica and Perry break out of an overly masculine **or** overly feminine paradigm, I encourage them to follow the Principle of Versatility. The word "versatility" comes from the Latin word versa, which means "to turn." The Principle of Versatility is to turn between masculine "push energy" and feminine "pull energy" to solve problems as needed. When you practice the Versatility Principle, you intentionally and strategically apply the masculine or the feminine principle based on the task at hand. Leaders cognizant of the downsides of being too masculine or too feminine follow the Versatility Principle to blend the best of both styles of leadership.

The Principle of Versatility unleashes the power of masculine *and* feminine energy by

- Factoring in facts *and* feelings into conversations
- Allowing people to build on each other's ideas
- Being inclusive *and* selective about who to engage in the decision-making process
- Respecting lines of authority while empowering people to reach across them
- Alternating push *and* pull energy to move ideas from "me to we"

With the Principle of Versatility, you don't end up with forced or fake alignment; you achieve *true* alignment.

"Check your ego at the door. The ego can be the great success inhibitor. It can kill opportunities, and it can kill success."

DWAYNE JOHNSON

The shift to a versatile way of leading must start with you. To break out of the confines of the masculine principle you must check your ego at the door. The ego is attached to getting attention and recognition for ideas. As you include others, your ego will continually insist that by letting others in on your brilliant ideas, you risk becoming dispensable, or worse, invisible. But the opposite is true. By letting go of the need to control and own every aspect of your ideas, your power grows exponentially with each person who becomes a part of the plan.

Too often, we confuse seeking validation with seeking alignment. For alignment to work well, let go of the need to have the right or best answer. If you find yourself getting easily offended when people don't agree with you, don't blame them. You likely have an ego problem. When it comes to tapping into the brilliance of co-creation, ego is not your friend; it is your enemy. Ego management is hard work. If you find that your ego is in your way, I recommend reading the book *Ego is the Enemy* by Ryan Holiday.

On the other hand, if you are stuck within the confines of the feminine principle, you may not give yourself or others permission to stand out. As Marianne Williamson writes in her book, *A Return to Love*, "Your playing small doesn't serve anyone." Alignment works best when creative impulses are honored and given a spotlight. If you don't allow for some authorship of ideas, then the path to alignment will feel like a three-legged race and you won't leverage the unique brilliance of your players.

Using the Versatility Principle as your leadership operating system makes sense, no matter your gender identity. However, subconscious cultural and gender bias often leads us to overvalue one side of the equation. Leaders who follow the Versatility Principle transcend stereotypes and move ideas from "me to we" to create balanced, inclusive, and satisfying solutions for all while also staying true to themselves.

In today's volatile and fast-moving world, the workplace requires the talents of men and women combined. When we intentionally tap into the full range of masculine and feminine strengths by leaning into the Versatility Principle, we deliver more value to customers, more profits to shareholders, and create a balanced workplace where all can thrive.

Following the Versatility Principle can be challenging at times. Subconscious gender biases often hold us back, and some work cultures are mired in a masculine or feminine paradigm that can be hard to break out of. That said, the practices of alignment, including the 4 Steps of Alignment and the 5 Cs of Feedback presented in the next section of this book are all founded on the Versatility Principle. If you follow these practices, you will naturally become a more versatile leader and play a role in creating a versatile culture on your team.

To learn more about our theory of versatility, visit our website www.VersatilityFactor.com.

SECTION 2. MEMORABLE SUCCESS FORMULAS

- True alignment is never forced or faked
- Practice Iterative Co-creation
- People don't take down what they build
- When it comes to innovation, iteration is your friend
- Efficiency is too small a god to serve

- Double down on SHUVA
- Masculine + Feminine = Versatility
- Creativity is crushed when rushed
- Ego is your enemy
- Move ideas from “me to we”

SECTION 3

THE 4 STEPS AND 5 Cs OF ALIGNMENT

Have you ever thought to yourself, *"I wish I could get X to do ________?"* Whether the X is your direct report who never seems to come through or a big group that feels tough to wrangle, the good news is you are only four steps away from that wish coming true.

The path to any agreement is meandering, yet predictable. Every conversation that leads to alignment starts from divergent thinking and moves toward convergent thinking. However, this progression can be chaotic and painful. When ideas emerge, they tend to bounce around like a pinball. This runs the risk of good ideas never "scoring" and instead just falling down the gobble hole. When groups stay in divergent thinking for too long, people just give up and it's "game over."

Leading divergent thinking is easy; it's getting the group to converge that's hard. Instead of letting the conversation go unstructured, use a standard process to efficiently funnel ideas from divergence to convergence. That process is the 4 Steps of Alignment.

The 4 Steps of Alignment are:

Propose

Probe

Re-Propose

Close

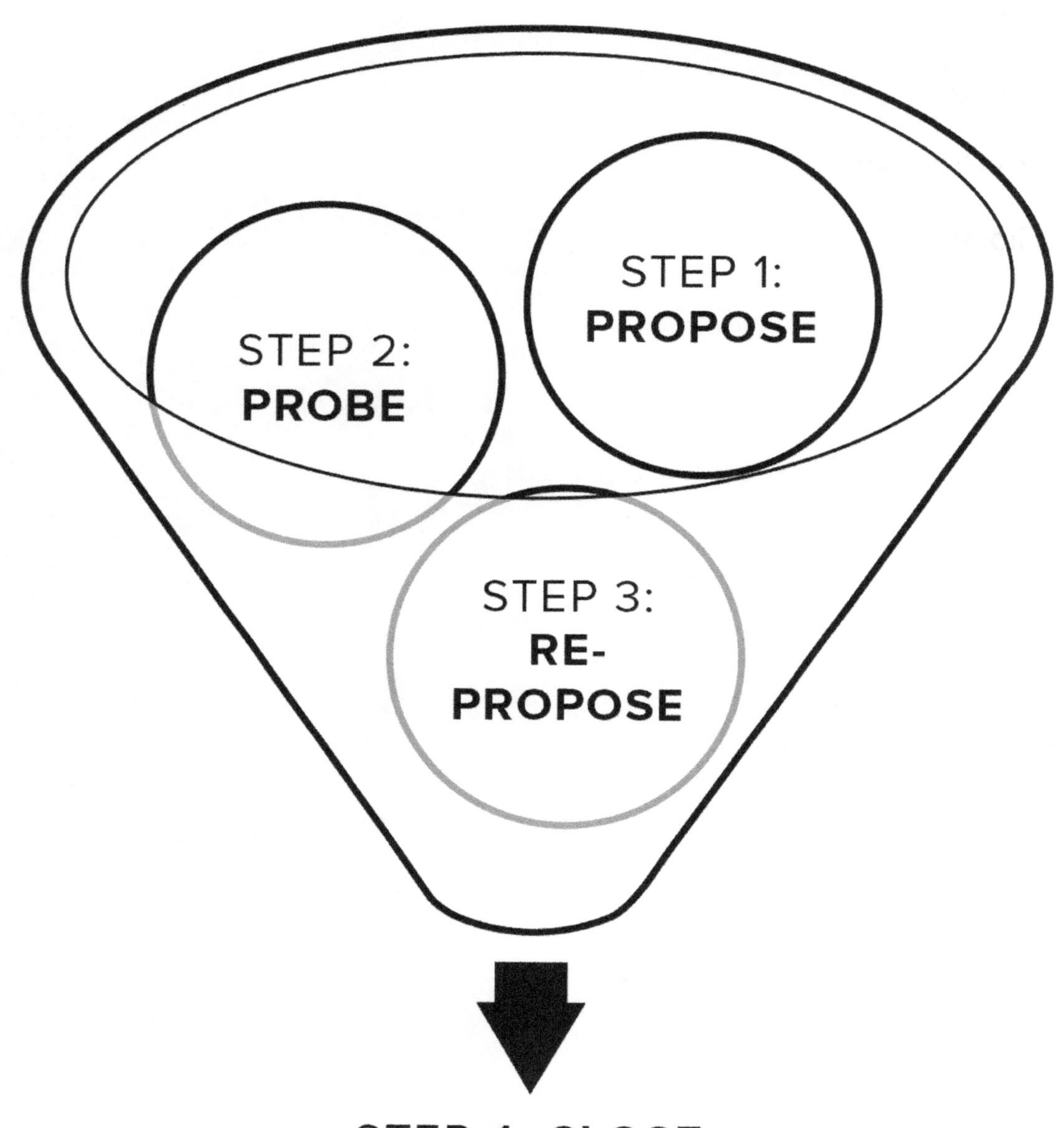

PROPO SE	A simple proposal is presented as an informal draft to the group for deliberation.

PROBE	The group gathers feedback using 4 of the 5 Cs (Clarifications, Compliments, Concerns, and Changes) to improve upon the proposal.
RE-PROPOSE	After taking a break to integrate the feedback collected so far into a second version of the proposal, the second version is presented to the group. The group is then tested for the 5th C—Commitment—using polling. Suggestions for changes are made until the desired level of agreement is achieved.
CLOSE	The leader finalizes the agreement verbally or in writing and sends documentation to all key stakeholders.

The 4 Steps of Alignment can be used casually between two people or formally with a large group. Whether you are working with one or many, I encourage you to follow the four steps in order so you can see for yourself how well it works. To help everyone follow along, make the 4 Steps visible. A one-page cheat sheet of the 4 Steps is available in the Appendix and can be downloaded from our website at www.leadershipsmarts.com/alignment

CHAPTER 6

STEP 1

PROPOSE

"To change the world, you don't have to be perfect; all you need is an idea worth sharing and worth following."

—FREDERICK J.B. MOORE II

Committed conversation is conversation *for* something and includes a commitment to accountability. For example, a committed conversation could begin, "We should ask our customers for leads for sales," followed by action steps. In this case, both the speaker and the listener are engaged, accountable, and moving toward something.

Contrast this with uncommitted conversation in which people have no accountability, which is characterized by statements such as, "Maybe we should revamp our website," or "We should have revised our website ages ago!" Conversations about an issue are uncommitted conversations. Uncommitted conversation is conversation *about* something, and its participants have no intention to take action on what they are talking about.

The act of making a proposal shifts the conversation from uncommitted to committed and from divergent to convergent thinking. Just be careful not to go too far. Proposals are NOT declarations. When it comes to alignment, *declarations are deadly* because they leave no room for iterative co-creation. They set up challenges and power struggles and are off-putting.

PREPARING THE PROPOSAL

Sometimes formulating a proposal can be difficult, especially if the decision to be made is political. Furthermore, groups can get caught up in details and wordsmithing. For this reason, I am not a fan of generating a proposal in a group. Instead, I recommend formulating proposals individually before convening and then bringing them to the group for deliberation.

This can be done in one of two ways.

- Option 1. Make a proposal for the group yourself.
- Option 2. Ask someone in the group to come up with an initial proposal.

One advantage of delegating the proposal is that it creates a culture of empowerment by allowing for proposals to come from anyone. Sometimes the best ideas come from the "shop room floor," not the top of the house.

The proposal can be as simple as a page with a few bullet points. After all, the whole point of the 4 Steps is to improve the proposal. However, if you don't feel confident about what to propose, gather ideas from a wide circle using one-on-one conversations or crowdsourcing techniques.

HOLD A BRAINSTORMING SESSION

The key to brainstorming is to efficiently get as many ideas out on the table as possible. Simply convening a group and asking each person to come up with ideas does not work, according to research cited by Keith Sawyer, author of *Group Genius: The Creative Power of Collaboration.* For one thing, I've observed that in brainstorming sessions, the first ideas presented, as well as ideas from a person of authority, often bias all the ideas that follow or prevent the expression of an opposing view.

To prevent bias from shutting out good ideas in your brainstorming session, start your session by asking each person to reflect silently and write their ideas down on a card before sharing with the group. Then sort the cards into themes and prioritize them. To do this efficiently, first ask one person to share their idea and post it to a whiteboard, then ask if others had similar ideas on their cards. Collect cards from those people and place them near the first card. Then ask another person to share a new idea. Post the second idea, then group similar ideas with that card. Continue until all ideas are on the wall and organized into themes. This quickly and easily assembles affinity groups of ideas.

Then narrow the list themes using multivoting by giving each person in the group several votes. They can use all of their votes on one idea if they feel that strongly about it, or they can distribute their votes over several items. This makes the degree of commitment to ideas more visible.

RUN AN ONLINE SURVEY

To gather ideas from many people, your best option is an online survey. These are a cinch when you use free tools like Google

Forms and Survey Monkey. In a short time, you can gather ideas from hundreds, even thousands of people and assemble them into a data table that allows you to sort and find themes. However, if you prefer a more low-tech approach, you can also make a personal appeal for ideas through email or social media.

HOST A FOCUS GROUP

A focus group is a small but demographically diverse group of stakeholders invited to share their reactions to an idea or product. Questions are asked in an interactive group setting where participants are free to talk with other group members. During this process, the researcher takes notes to record the vital points.

The focus group gets you out of your echo chamber and can help you anticipate which ideas others will favor. However, if you find it too hard to convene a group, you can hold brief, private sessions to gather feedback and ideas instead.

While these suggestions provide a start for crowdsourcing ideas, for more creative methods, my go-to resource is *The Surprising Power of Liberating Structures: Simple Rules to Unleash a Culture of Innovation* (2016) by Henri Lipmanowicz and Keith McCandless.

Use these methods to generate ideas, then write them up into a simple singular proposal that highlights the best or most popular idea.

HOW TO WRITE A GOOD PROPOSAL

Once you have narrowed down ideas into a preferred option, you are ready to create your proposal or to delegate the task to someone else. Remember, a proposal is like a first date; you aren't married yet, so don't get too attached. "Bad proposals" move the group forward just as well as good ones because they help the group discover what they don't like.

KEEP IT SIMPLE

A good proposal is not a polished pitch to sell someone on something. Bring forward something you haven't spent too much time on so that you aren't too attached to it. This type of proposal is often called a straw-dog proposal. The goal is to generate discussion of its advantages and disadvantages and provoke the generation of new and better proposals. Remember, your proposal is made of straw, not stone, so you can tear it apart and rebuild it.

KEEP IT SHORT

If a proposal is too long and complex, it will be difficult for the group to process. One to two pages is about the most information your team can consider effectively in one session. Rule of thumb: make your proposal so simple it can "fit on the back of a napkin." If your proposal is more complicated than that, break it down into back-of-a-napkin-sized chunks.

RULE OF 3S

The best proposals use the Rule of 3s: always limit your messages to three main points. The Rule of 3s is based on research proving that people can only remember three points after a presentation. If you present more than three ideas, you run the risk that one point will be forgotten later. The Rule of 3s focuses energy on what is most important. If necessary, you can add another level of detail by breaking down the three main points into three sub-points each. If you follow the Rule of 3s, you will be amazed at how easy it can be for your team members to consider, internalize, and remember your ideas.

DON'T BE FUZZY

Good proposals should be specific enough that people can visualize them. A handy test is to make sure your proposals address the five W's: who, what, when, where, and why. By providing an adequate level of detail, you give the group something concrete to react to. Don't fall into the trap of overgeneralizing to avoid a negative reaction. Remember, the goal is to elicit reactions and opinions from the group ("Oh, I like this," or "I don't like this."). If your audience can't visualize the proposal, the conversation will not be very lively.

Fuzzy proposal example:

"I propose that we use a marketing plan to guide our decisions."

Specific proposal example:

"I propose…

1. Al and Susan come up with a marketing plan by December 1.
2. we use their marketing plan to guide decisions about our website revision and
3. we also use it to inform our year-end email campaign."

In the fuzzy example, it would be easy for the group to nod and agree, but it runs the risk that nothing will happen or that the team will create a marketing plan that doesn't impact the website or email projects.

PRESENTING THE PROPOSAL

It helps to provide a copy of the proposal before a session so your audience can become familiar with it. This is particularly helpful for introverts who need time to internally process ideas before sharing their opinions publicly. Be sure to let the group know that what you're presenting is just a working draft. Write (or watermark) the words "DRAFT FOR DISCUSSION" on every page. If you don't, your draft might be misinterpreted as a premature final decision and prompt a lot of negative reactions before you ever get the chance to present it.

I learned this lesson the hard way. I once consulted for a nonprofit board that commissioned a committee to make recommendations for governance changes. The committee prepared a simple presentation for an alignment session with the board and sent out the recommendation in the board package. Unfortunately, many board members believed they were reading a final recommendation. When the meeting started, it felt like the villagers had shown up with pitchforks and torches. We wasted over half an hour convincing them that the circulated copy was not a final decision, and instead was just step one in gathering feedback. Don't let this happen to you!

If you don't circulate a copy before the meeting, be sure to provide printed copies in the meeting so attendees can follow along and take notes. It is also helpful to project the proposal visually using slides or a flipchart.

When presenting a proposal, use the language, "I propose..." to take ownership of what you are moving toward. The words "I propose" send a powerful linguistic signal that we are moving out of uncommitted conversation into committed conversation.

Next, “walk through” the proposal at a high level *before* opening the conversation for questions or comments. This allows for a cohesive picture to emerge in the minds of the participants. Explain that time for feedback will come next in Step 2, the Probe Step, and ask your participants to hold off on questions and comments and instead to take notes as they listen.

CHAPTER 7

STEP 2

PROBE

"The key to wisdom is this—constant and frequent questioning, for by doubting, we are led to question, by questioning we arrive at the truth."

—PETER ABELARD

In the Probe step of the process, we engage the audience in the work of improving the proposal. When we gather reactions in a logical order, we make the emergent collective thinking as transparent as possible. Collective thinking is the act of gathering all ideas, even if they are opposing, trusting that eventually, a preferred option will emerge. Collective thinking should not be confused with groupthink, which is what happens when no one challenges the leader or the most popular idea. Let your group know that you encourage them to share all views and that dissent is good for the group. The Probe step is when everyone gets a voice.

It is not unusual for ideas to be presented followed by an open-ended question such as, "Reactions?" or "What do you think?" In my experience, this method of probing can go wrong in two ways. The first is that it can result in radio silence or a meaningless affirmative answer like, "Sounds good." What appears to be agreement is just complacency.

The second most likely thing to occur is the pinball game, where ideas bounce around and get batted at but eventually just roll down the hole only to be followed by another round of balls.

Instead of probing in a random way, collect feedback using four of the 5 Cs: Clarifications, Compliments, Concerns, and Changes, in that exact order. First, ask Clarifying questions. Next, encourage Compliments about the proposal. Then you are ready to explore Concerns and Changes that can resolve the Concerns. Finally, test for the last C—Commitment.

Here are a few tips about the Probe step…

1. The audience will want to jump ahead. Don't let that happen; instead, hold the line and make sure they follow the Cs in the right order.
2. Give participants a notepad to capture what they are thinking so they can hold on to ideas and share them when the right time comes.
3. Make sure someone is transcribing all comments (using the template in the Appendix or on a flipchart).

5 Cs FEEDBACK

CLARIFICATIONS

Are you familiar with the Old Testament story of the Tower of Babel? The Babylonians wanted to build a tower tall enough to reach heaven, but to smite the Babylonians for their hubris, God cursed the tower builders by making them speak different languages so they could not understand each other. Thus, they could never complete their tower.

These days most projects require that cross-functional teams come together to "build a tower." It is not unusual for each function to speak a unique language full of jargon and acronyms that other functions don't understand. If your project crosses lines of technical discipline (e.g., sales and ops or engineering and finance), make sure a language barrier does not impede understanding.

To avoid the curse of Babylon, always start with Clarifications. Clarifications are needed for two reasons: either you have used jargon or acronyms that are not as widely shared as you would think, or your terms are too general. Clarifying questions clear up points of confusion so that participants can provide useful feedback.

Start the clarification process by asking open-ended questions such as: "What do we need to clarify to make sure you understand where I'm going here?" If you get no reaction, you may ask people to imagine what clarifications an external audience who didn't know the "lingo" might need. This will help those who are embarrassed that they need clarification feel like they are helping by pointing out areas of potential confusion.

Avoid posing a yes or no question, such as "Do you need any clarifications?" That generally results in short yes or no answers, and silence from any audience members who may be embarrassed to admit they don't understand the proposal.

I will warn you now; people won't want to start with clarifying questions. Instead, they will want to jump into Concerns or Changes right out of the gate. When they do, HOLD THE LINE. Patiently and proactively redirect them to save those ideas for later in the process.

Be a stickler and listen carefully for their attempts to disguise Concerns and Changes as clarifications.

Here are some examples:

CLARIFYING QUESTIONS	NOT CLARIFYING QUESTIONS
"When you said, 'marketing plan,' which one were you referencing?	"Shouldn't we focus on strategy before marketing?" (thinly veiled Change)
"Can you explain the cost and timeline for moving our equipment?"	"Isn't it disruptive to move our equipment?" (thinly veiled Concern)
"What is your rationale for including three features?"	"Shouldn't we have more than three features?" (thinly veiled Concern)
"I see you are suggesting we use Salesforce CRM. What does CRM stand for?"	"I see you are suggesting using Salesforce CRM. Isn't Zoho CRM a better option?" (thinly veiled Change)

Instruct the group to only ask questions to make sure they understand what you have presented. This is not the time for expressing an opinion, a preference, or a reservation.

For example, you might say, "It's important to stick to Clarifications, as later we will have the opportunity to discuss Concerns and Changes. It's okay to ask why I chose Salesforce to clarify the rationale, but it's not time to introduce another option, Concern or Change—please hold that for later."

By the time you finish clarifications, you should have cleared up any misunderstandings and filled in missing information. Be generous, even if you think your proposal covers things you feel you've already said a hundred times that everyone should know by now. Don't get frustrated when Clarifications take longer than you expected.

Instead, budget time for Clarifications and be grateful for the opportunity to create the possibility of true alignment by building a common language and understanding.

COMPLIMENTS

Asking the group to Compliment the merits of the proposal presented is the secret ingredient in the 5 Cs recipe. While you may have been taught that it is improper to fish for Compliments, I couldn't disagree more! Never skip Compliments! No matter who proposes, including yourself, take the time to ask what people like about the proposal. This is as simple as asking the question: "What do you like about what is being proposed?"

This simple act injects SHUVA into the room and creates the goodwill needed to move toward the risky next step in the process: expressing Concerns. It goes a long way toward creating psychological safety, not only for the presenter but also for the audience. Also, knowing what works gets you one step closer to alignment. If half the proposal is good, you are halfway to agreement. Pointing this out can keep the presenter and group from getting discouraged if it seems like the proposal needs a lot of work. I have seen meetings where an overwhelmingly popular proposal was presented, but most of the conversation that followed focused on one detail that wasn't perfect. The proposer walked away feeling rejected, even though the audience was satisfied with almost all of the proposal.

Far too many groups are stingy about talking about what they like. If being complimentary isn't the norm in your group, complimenting someone might feel disingenuous. But you will be surprised at how quickly groups get good at this and how much they come to enjoy it.

You may have a group that wants to skip this step and cut to the chase to work on the creative part of revealing Concerns and Changes. If this is the case, I recommend that you insist that at least two or three compliments be shared before the group moves on to Concerns. For instance, you can say, "Let's make sure that Helen's hard work gets acknowledged. Let's hear from at least two people: what part of the proposal do you like?"

Compliments should always come before Concerns or Changes. A way to remember this is the adage, *"Always praise the baby before you raise the baby."* If someone were introducing their child to you, you would never start by saying, "Wow, Johnny sure has a big mouth; you better save up for braces!" Instead, you would find something wonderful to share about the baby. Normalize sharing what you like about a proposal before sharing Concerns or Changes. This practice goes a long way toward creating a SHUVA environment for the proposer and psychological safety for all. If you practice making sure every proposal receives complimentary feedback, innovation will steadily increase because your teammates will know the group appreciates their initiative.

CONCERNS

After clarifications and compliments, it's time for Concerns. Concerns are necessary risk factors mentioned out of a desire to be helpful. Concerns are *not* criticisms or complaints. When we were naming the Cs, we chose the word Concerns because it comes from a caring frame of mind, whereas criticism comes from a judgmental or faultfinding frame of mind. That makes all the difference.

Expressing Concerns allows for doubts and reservations that might lead to the proposal's rejection. That's okay. The possibility of "no" should always be a part of your group's process of reaching a final decision. As Peter Block says in his book, *Community: The Structure of Belonging,* "If you can't say no, your yes means nothing."

Always give people a chance to express dissent. This is the only way they can clarify how the proposal might impact their area of interest or work.

Invite people to share concerns using open-ended questions like:

- "What Concerns do you have about what is being proposed?"
- "What risks do we need to consider about what is being proposed?"

If the proposal presented isn't all that fabulous, the group will likely be eager to share their Concerns. If this is the case, double down on SHUVA and lean into it. Sometimes leaders don't want to invite Concerns because they fear doing so might undermine their credibility or expose vulnerabilities in their proposal. They might then do an end-run by asking a cursory yes/no question like, "Any concerns?" Again, these closed questions tend to get the "Nope, all good." superficial answer.

Don't fall for that. When you encourage people to fully express Concerns, you show them their opinions are valued. Furthermore, knowing Concerns allows you to address them before taking action. Often Concerns are based on misconceptions that you can straighten out once they are expressed.

If a person appears rattled when they bring up a Concern, take a little extra time to explore their energy. You might say something like: "It looks like this is important to you and maybe even upsetting;

could you please elaborate a bit on what is coming up for you now?" This is another way to offer SHUVA and build psychological safety.

If the concerns expressed are so serious that they kill the proposal, remember that it is still a big win! Killing a misguided proposal prevents you from wasting time on something doomed to fail.

If there are no Concerns, and audience members say, "No, it's awesome," don't fall for that. Instead, say, "Well, let's just double-check. If there *were* any Concerns here, what might they be?" This will send the signal it is safe to express Concerns.

Sometimes when Concerns come up, it makes sense to skip ahead to Changes. This will generally happen organically as people will say things like, "I'm concerned we're doing this on a Wednesday when there is no parking; let's change it to Thursday." It never hurts to say, "Do you have a suggested Change that would resolve your Concern? If so, hold it for Changes later."

Combining Concerns with Changes is one of the only times I allow for the 5 Cs to be explored out of order. However, if someone has a Concern but no idea how to address it, I don't push them to provide a solution. A popular leadership belief is that Concerns without solutions are not helpful. I disagree with this approach, as I think it just shuts down dialogue. Not all problems have clear answers. If we wait until we have a solution, we run the risk that the problem will become the elephant in the room.

CHANGES

This is where the magic happens. Some Changes are minor tweaks; others, huge leaps forward. At this point, it can be helpful to either provide a break or put people in small groups to generate ideas for Changes that will resolve the Concerns just discussed. Allow a “bulge” in your timeline in case this step activates the creative energy of the group. That way, you have time to explore emergent ideas.

You may need to limit the exploration of Changes due to time constraints. If too many ideas emerge, or if suggested Changes are diametrically opposed, poll the group to find the preferred option and steer things in that direction. If two options are tied, ask their advocates to make a case, then run the poll again. The goal is not to please everyone but to land on the option most likely to be adopted by all involved.

THE FIFTH C—COMMITMENT

Once you have explored the first four of the 5 Cs: Clarifications, Compliments, Concerns, and Changes, your Probe Step is complete. You now have all you need to formulate a good Re-proposal that integrates all the feedback shared thus far.

Once the Re-proposal is on the table, you are ready to test for the fifth C—Commitment—and achieve the level of agreement you desire.

CHAPTER 8

STEP 3

RE-PROPOSE

The Re-proposal step provides a clear picture of how the views of the group have led to a better proposal that can now be finalized. The closer you are to a final decision, the more things "get real," so get ready for a few plot turns.

If the suggested Changes are minimal, you may be able to create a suitable re-proposal on the fly. However, in most cases, you will need a long break to integrate all the feedback into a better proposal. For this reason, I prefer to cover the 4 Steps of Alignment in two sessions. The first session covers Propose and Probe; the second, Re-Propose and Close. Between sessions, plan enough time to write up the re-proposal, circulate it to participants, and give everyone a chance to "sleep on it."

The re-proposal should include the ideas that most resonated with the group, not everything that anyone expressed. Lean toward those ideas shared by decision-makers, informed experts, and those responsible for implementing solutions. Give the preferences of these key stakeholders more weight than those of people the final decision only casually impacts.

If the group has provided feedback that steers the proposal in a direction you have serious concerns about, you have two options. You can either accept the wisdom of the crowd and present a re-proposal that aligns with their views, or follow your own judgment and reject the feedback. Going against the crowd is generally a bad idea and should be done with caution and only if you have veto power.

Before going against the wisdom of the crowd, check your ego first. Are you unhappy that your original idea might have been lost? If your ego is in check, and you still feel that the most popular ideas present a serious risk, you may override the group if you hold the authority to do so. Just be aware there is a high price to pay, as it will impair your ability to get people to support your future alignment efforts.

A way to present the re-proposal would be, "I really appreciate all the ideas shared. We discussed the merits of ideas x and y, and it seems the majority favors y. Still, I have decided to move forward with x because (your rationale)."

Generally speaking, if you want the group you are working with to not only back the final decision but to actually own the outcome, don't ignore their insights. Do your best to find a way to create a re-proposal that reflects the wisdom of the crowd.

TESTING FOR COMMITMENT

Ideally, in this phase, the proposal gets a "Hell yes!" from everyone involved. That said, not every decision or plan requires an all-in level of Commitment from every decision-maker and stakeholder. Sometimes a lesser level of agreement is enough to move forward. The nuances of defining the desired level of agreement are more fully explained in chapter 10, Initial Considerations. The holy grail of alignment is to get everyone to the highest level of agreement possible. And I don't mean "I can live with it," agreement. I mean "YES, let's do this!" Commitment.

No matter what level of agreement you are shooting for, you need to read the room accurately and get each person to fully express their Commitment level. Don't just take nodding heads as a sign of Commitment. Instead, run a Commitment test. I recommend that you use a way for people to verbally and physically show Commitment. This is a much better way to seal the deal than just asking, "So, is everybody in?" Using our body to signal our level of Commitment engages whole-body intelligence, which often holds wisdom that our brains do not. In an informal alignment session, you can test Commitment by asking a question like, "On a scale of one to ten, how excited are you about this proposal?" This question can provoke thinking, especially when followed up by a question like, "What can we do to make it a ten for you?"

When working with a larger group, it is helpful to use a more efficient process to test the Commitment level of the group. My favorite method is called "Fist to Five" polling.

FIST TO FIVE POLLING

Fist to Five polling is a deceptively simple technique that software development teams use to poll members. The facilitator asks the team to use their hands to show their level of support for the initial proposal. Each team member responds by holding up a closed fist or the number of fingers that corresponds to their level of support. The more fingers up, the higher the level of support.

CLOSED FIST
I must block this.

3 FINGERS
I'm not a fan, but okay with it.

1 FINGER
I can't stand it.

4 FINGERS
I'm on board.

2 FINGERS
I think it still needs work.

5 FINGERS
I'm on fire, let's do this!

When I conduct Fist to Five polls, I ask all the participants to put their heads down, then I say, "Rock, paper, scissors, shoot," to signal it is time to throw up their hands to vote. I do this to help each person express their own view without being swayed by how others are voting.

Once all hands are in the air, I ask the audience to lift their heads to see how the vote landed. If there are a lot of people in the room, you can start by asking fives to hold their hands high, then drop them, fours next, and so on.

If the Fist to Five poll doesn't reveal a room of threes or higher, the level of agreement is still pretty low. When this happens, encourage people to share the rationale for their level of Commitment. What I usually do is call on someone at the high end to share the reason why they are such a strong proponent of the re-proposal. Then I ask for someone at the low end to share their Concerns and what Changes might move them into a higher level of agreement. Often, the low-end person will suggest a super useful Change.

I usually use the Fist to Five polling method several times. I run the poll, then ask for someone on the high and someone on the low end to express their views, then poll again. Usually, these steps move the group toward the most popular view, but sometimes, they can flip the vote in a new direction.

Often, the closer you are to making a decision, the more people are willing to share doubts and reservations they previously kept to themselves. More than once, I've had a room full of fours and fives with only one person at a one or two. When the low-end person shared their Concern with courage and conviction, they convinced the entire room to move toward their point of view. That might seem like a negative outcome, but I disagree. In those cases, deciding not to take an action that had grown popular but had serious risk factors was absolutely the best outcome.

An example of this occurred when I was working with a group of twelve senior managers who were considering moving the data management function from Colorado to Maryland to be closer to clients in D.C. When they did the Fist to Five poll, eleven out of the twelve were voting at a level of four or five in favor of the proposed relocation. Only one person, Chris, was holding out at a level two. Now Chris was on the hot seat, the lone wolf preventing a consensus from being reached. I knew that if I didn't handle it right, Chris might cave in without revealing his true misgivings. After so much work, I didn't want to settle for fake alignment, so I doubled down on SHUVA and said, "Chris, I know it's hard to go against the crowd this late in the game. Your opinion matters, so please feel free to share what has you voting so low."

Chris then explained how hard it was to attract data managers. When his last data manager was poached by a competitor, it took six months to replace him. Not only would it be hard to hire the talent needed in Maryland, the Colorado data managers in high-demand would not relocate since they could easily find new jobs in their hometown. Chris had already mentioned the tight labor market, but for some reason, it didn't click with the rest of the group until now. When I asked for someone to advocate in favor of relocation, no one volunteered. So, I took another Fist to Five poll. This time, all the mangers had flipped and were now at a level two. So, despite the downside of working with clients remotely, the decision was made to keep the Colorado office in place.

You can continue using Fist to Five polling to test for Commitment and then deliberate the gap until you've reached the desired level of agreement. If you've done a thorough job in the Probe step, this should go fast, but you may have to cycle back through the Probe and Re-propose steps a few times if the gap between those in favor and those not yet willing to commit is too wide.

Before you move on, be sure to issue a "last call." Use a statement like this:

> "By now, we've thoroughly deliberated this topic and are coming to a close. Before we finalize our decision, this is your last call to express any lingering Concerns or desired Changes. Please speak now as it really isn't fair to bring up Concerns after we've disassembled. Now is your chance. Keep in mind that once the final decision is made, we all own it, even if what we decided was not your preference. Once the decision is made, we expect your full Commitment."

If you don't issue the last call, you risk having team members waiting until they get to the water cooler to deep-six all your hard work. Training your team to speak up is one of the big benefits of using the

4 Steps of Alignment. It can break the bad habit of passive-aggressive behaviors that derail alignment.

Once you have completed the re-proposal and the last call, you are ready to move on to the last step of alignment, Close.

CHAPTER 9

STEP 4

CLOSE

All too often, we neglect to Close properly. We kick the can down the road, postponing decisions to a later date. This can be a big waste of time and creates a perpetual churn. So, finalize your agreement by declaring a formal close; that doesn't mean the topic can never be reopened, but it does signal an intent to commit and move into action.

TIPS FOR CLOSING

You've reached the Close when all parties have reached the desired level of agreement. Resist the temptation to continue debating until everyone is 100 percent satisfied unless you really need that level of agreement. Closing should feel very satisfying and can even be acknowledged with applause and a bow. I often like to have a video of fireworks handy to project on a screen.

WHAT TO DO IF YOU CAN'T REACH AGREEMENT

Sometimes, you have gotten this far, and you still don't have a majority of people in agreement. In this case, you have three options for how to Close.

1. Realize you don't have the will forces behind the proposal to make it work and shelve the proposal.
2. Ask for volunteers to work up a new proposal to be revisited at a later date.
3. Acknowledge that you have areas of misalignment and ask the whole group to back up the chosen course of action anyway. This is the best choice if you are facing a tight deadline and must take action. Let the group know that failure is an option and that sometimes you just have to accept a suboptimum solution and see if you can make it work. Many call this way of closing before consensus is reached "to disagree and commit."

Be sure to nail down the Close, so people get that you won't be revisiting the decision later. It can be helpful to say something like, "Now that we are at Close, the train has left the station. Everyone on board needs to stay on board. We can't have anyone jump off after we have left the station." This will help "train the group" (pun intended) not to undermine decisions made later.

ALWAYS DOCUMENT

After you have declared the Close, it is important to document your final plan in writing and send it out to all stakeholders.

If you follow the 4 Steps of Alignment, you will find that good ideas become great ideas, and poor ideas are avoided. This process will improve the cohesion of the team and ownership of the outcome.

SECTION 3. MEMORABLE SUCCESS FORMULAS

- 4 Steps of Alignment: Propose, Probe, Re-propose, Close
- When it comes to alignment, declarations are deadly
- 5 Cs Feedback: Clarifications, Compliments, Concerns, Changes, and Commitment
- Compliments always come before Concerns ("always praise the baby before you raise the baby")
- Use Fist to Five polling to test for the fifth C (Commitment)
- Make sure everyone is on board before the train leaves the station

SECTION 4

PREPARING FOR ALIGNMENT

"By failing to prepare, you are preparing to fail."

—BENJAMIN FRANKLIN

In this section, we provide tips on how to prepare for alignment when you have a large or complex project that involves many stakeholders. Before starting your efforts to align stakeholders, there are a few things you should think through and plan out to set everyone up for success.

CHAPTER 10

INITIAL CONSIDERATIONS

Stephen Covey, the author of *The 7 Habits of Highly Effective People: Powerful Lessons in Personal Change*, says, "Always start with the end in mind." This is especially true when it comes to aligning others; if they can see a clear picture of what needs to be achieved and why it matters, this will go a long way toward pointing them in the same direction.

When you set the direction, you must clarify the desired outcome, not the steps to achieve it. For example, "We need to get the floor so clean, it shines," is a clear outcome to pursue. However, "We need to sweep the floor, then mop the floor," is not an outcome; it is a series of steps. By clarifying desired outcomes rather than the steps to achieve them, you leave room for people to work with you co-creatively to figure out how to get the job done.

If possible, describe the end goal using a tangible metric and be sure to clarify why that metric matters. For example, I'm working to grow my business ten-fold over the next three years. As I work with my team, we are all motivated by the idea that we can improve the lives of ten times as many managers as we currently serve. We will improve not only those managers' lives, but also the lives of those who report to them. This gives each person on the team plenty of room to propose how they will contribute to that goal over the years using the 4 Steps of Alignment.

Our end goal may not be realistic. This is by design. When you set a goal, it's important to be bold. Don't limit yourself to what's currently realistic. Instead, use "moonshot thinking." Aim to achieve something generally believed to be impossible. Moonshot thinking frames all problems as solvable and encourages "anything is possible" dialogues around how to approach challenges. When you strive beyond current reality toward a noble ideal, you provoke creativity and fresh thinking. For example, reaching for an aspirational goal of zero waste in manufacturing is much more compelling than reaching for a 20 percent reduction in waste. Even if you don't achieve your moonshot target, you are likely to achieve an outcome you previously thought was beyond your current limits.

I once worked with Ian, an IT manager whose team had the job of installing complex information security systems in healthcare clinics. The security installation took three months and was highly disruptive to the clinic's productivity. Ian set a moonshot goal of getting installations down from three months to three weeks within one year. His team was inspired by this call to action and used the 4 Steps of Alignment to come up with great ideas that shortened installation times without impacting the quality of the system installed. At the end of the year, they astounded themselves and their customers by lowering installation time to four weeks. They missed the three-week goal, but four weeks was still well beyond what anyone ever thought possible. The win was so remarkable that Ian was soon promoted to head-up all IT installations.

A word of caution about setting moonshot goals. Never punish anyone for not meeting a stretch goal. If you do, moonshots will be demoralizing. If you set a moonshot goal, don't be too disappointed if it is not met. Make sure to celebrate even small wins.

DEFINE WHERE TO START

Sometimes it can be difficult to know where to start the process of alignment. Should you start at the top and work down or at the bottom and work up? The best approach, when possible, is to convene all stakeholders for deliberations at the same time. By convening all stakeholders, you minimize iterations and speed up the process. However, this is not always possible or practical. In that case, start with the most informed and involved players. Once the key stakeholders are in motion toward alignment, you can expand to additional stakeholder groups to build on the initial momentum.

I began coaching one client, Brad, a few weeks after he started as CEO of a nonprofit arts organization. The search for a new CEO had been long, and the large board and staff had put off making any decisions while the hiring process dragged on.

Brad knew that his organization needed strategic direction right away. But he was unsure how to best engage the talents of his board, staff, and donors—and he didn't know where to start. The board was technically in charge of setting the strategic direction, but most members were not in touch with the day-to-day realities of the organization. The staff was in touch with the realities but starting with them was risky because setting strategy was technically the board's job. And if he tried to work in parallel with both groups, he'd risk losing his own fresh ideas.

So, Brad started with himself. I encouraged him to organize his ideas using the Power of 3s and create a plan that could be explained on the back of a napkin. Next, Brad used the 4 Steps to refine the plan with his staff. He warned the staff that the plan would need to be approved by the board. Next, he emailed the plan to the board so that they could preview it before the board meeting. In the email, he let the board know that the plan was only a DRAFT and encouraged them to challenge it. The board didn't reject or challenge the plan, though. They embraced it. For the first time since the formation of the organization, they achieved alignment from top to bottom.

Whether you use a top-down or bottom-up approach, the key to success is the same. Follow the principles and the 4 Steps and know it will require many steps before all players are aligned.

DEFINING VOICE AND VOTE

A business is not a democracy where everyone gets a vote on every decision. Lines of authority exist for a reason. Not everyone has the time to get up to speed enough to offer an informed opinion on every topic. Furthermore, some players have more at stake than others. For this reason, it is important to clarify lines of authority *before* the alignment process starts by defining vote and voice. Votes that finalize a decision should be reserved for experts and those held accountable for the outcome. While being selective about who gets to vote to finalize a decision, be sure to give as many stakeholders as you can a voice. When you are generous about who gets a voice and selective about who gets a vote, you can move toward alignment in an *inclusive,* yet also practical way without bogging down the process.

If you have formal authority over a final decision, you may reserve the right to make the ultimate decision yourself. Or, you can delegate the vote to a smaller group of colleagues who have the time, energy, and expertise to be fully invested in the decision-making process. If you don't, then every decision will start to feel like a three-legged race.

This doesn't mean that others should not get a voice in the discussion that leads up to the vote. Even uninformed stakeholders can provide insights. Including more stakeholders helps more people end up fully informed and ready to move forward once you've finalized a decision. There are many ways to reach out so that no groups are left out. For example, you could have a single representative from each stakeholder group speak for their group as the process moves forward.

To be inclusive in a practical way, remember this MSF: *Everyone gets a voice, but not everyone gets a vote.*

It is key to let everyone know who has a vote and who only has a voice right from the get-go. Otherwise, people may assume they have authority over a decision because they were asked to provide feedback on an idea.

DEFINE THE LEVEL OF AGREEMENT

Once you have decided who gets a voice and who gets a vote, it is important to define the level of agreement needed for a decision to be finalized. There are many different levels of agreement, and the 4 Steps of Alignment can be used with all of them. The key to success is to clarify the level of agreement you are shooting for **before** you start the process.

Here are different levels of agreement:

CONCORDANCE

"Concord" means "agreement among persons; concurrence in attitudes, feelings, etc." The word "concordance" here refers to a decision with which everyone is 100 percent satisfied. While reaching concordance is ideal, it isn't always practical, especially if the group is large and time is limited. Generally, concordance is only necessary when power is split evenly between multiple parties, say, between two founders making a decision about a risky investment.

CONSENSUS

Consensus occurs when all parties in the room feel they can live with the agreement. It might not be the outcome they prefer, but they agree with it enough to stand behind it. Generally speaking, this is the level of agreement I try to reach for when I facilitate sessions.

MAJORITY RULE

Another fair way to make decisions is to choose a solution that satisfies the majority. While this approach is generally more robust than less inclusive approaches, it is also pretty risky. Majority rule runs the risk that a minority leaves very dissatisfied with the chosen path. Just a few dissenters can cause the decision to fall apart, so for that reason, I prefer to shoot for consensus or concordance and only settle for majority rule if we are up against a tight constraint like a serious deadline.

CONSULTATIVE

If you are in a position of authority, you might ask a few stakeholders to offer their counsel, while reserving the vote to yourself. By using this approach, you can enrich your thinking so that your decision is less likely to have unintended, negative consequences. Consultative decision-making is a weak approach to alignment but can work well, especially if the decision at hand is not controversial. Most stakeholders like being asked their opinion and will feel included even if your final decision doesn't align with their advice.

AUTHORITATIVE

If you are in a position of authority, you are accountable for the outcomes of decisions. Therefore, you should always reserve the right to override decisions your group favors. While it is not recommended, if you lead an alignment conversation and you are the only dissenter in the group, it is your prerogative to not follow the group's recommendation. If you choose this course of action, you do so at your own peril. Having asked your team for their view, you know you are proceeding without their full support.

DEFINE THE QUORUM

The minimum number of people who must be present to take a vote or finalize a decision is known as a quorum. When defining the level of agreement, be sure to also define what your group considers a quorum. For example, you might define your quorum as having at least 75 percent of decision-makers present and at least one person from each stakeholder group. If you convene a meeting and don't have enough present to meet the quorum, reschedule the meeting until you have sufficient representation of all constituents.

DEFINE CONSTRAINTS

Before seeking alignment, be sure to clarify constraints. For example, you may invite your team to come up with a plan to revamp the website, but implement constraints, such as limits on changes to the logo or how much can be spent on vendors.

Working toward alignment is like creating a funnel for ideas to move through. It helps to clarify if you are in a "wide funnel" or a "narrow funnel." When you have a lot of latitude to co-create the solution, you are working with a *wide funnel*, which means the participants have few, if any, constraints. Generally speaking, wide-funnel conversations allow for more creativity and can often lead to breakthroughs.

More often we are working with a "narrow funnel," meaning we have many constraints on factors like time, resources, manpower, funding, location, or equipment. Either way, it helps if the leader clarifies the size of the funnel from the start.

The wider you open the funnel, the more opportunity you create for innovation. "Whitespace" projects are those for which the field is wide open to formulate a solution. When you work in whitespace, you define a problem and invite the group to start from scratch to solve it. They can forge a new path forward, free from constraints of timelines, resources, technology, processes, and other factors. Starting a project from a whitespace mentality fosters innovative thinking and creativity. While whitespace projects are wonderfully freeing, they can also be challenging due to the inherent ambiguity of the call to action. The 4 Steps are a powerful tool to help you move from the freedom of whitespace to a coordinated plan.

Recently, I worked with Chris, a CEO who used a wide funnel approach to get his team to make bold recommendations that would save the company during a market downturn. He was aware that the simplest way to save money would have been to cut staff. So, the only constraint he set was that no jobs would be cut. All other options would be seriously considered. Without the fear of job loss, the group jumped into the challenge and came up with many creative ideas that helped them come out of the crisis stronger than ever before.

While it makes sense to open the funnel as wide as possible, in some cases, unavoidable constraints force you to work within a narrow funnel. This is the case when you have a new regulation or policy that requires full compliance. With no room to move, you may wonder why you should even go through the 4 Steps and be tempted to just send out the mandate by email. If you do this, don't be surprised when no one follows the new rule.

Instead, use the 4 Steps to proactively align your team on the tasks they must do. This will give you a better sense of whether they are likely to comply with the new rule or not, and you can help them better understand the consequences of noncompliance.

Let's take, for example, the need to get your team to comply with a rule that could have serious legal consequences if broken. Holding an alignment session on the new rule can help your team feel in control and understand what is required of them. There is almost always some degree of wiggle room in how to follow a rule. For example, if the new rule is to wear a face mask, the 4 Steps might clarify exactly when the mask must be worn and any exceptions that might be allowed. Your team may see that a "dumb rule" actually has some merits. If indeed, the rule is onerous, you can also come up with creative ideas that will make the task less burdensome, such as offering a prize when a milestone is hit.

As you can see, initial considerations sometimes take as long as the alignment process itself. However, don't take them lightly. The more thought you put into the initial considerations reviewed above, the better off you will be in the long run.

CHAPTER 11

DEFINING THE PLAYERS

"Leadership can be defined in one word—honesty. You must be honest with the players and honest with yourself."

—EARL WEAVER

One thing that can be hard to determine is who to include on your path to alignment. To help you figure that out, map all stakeholders and consider the best approaches to including them.

STAKEHOLDER MAPPING

Before deciding who to include, step back and map out all parties who will be impacted by the change you need alignment around. These are your stakeholders. For example, if I want to launch a new video game, the stakeholders would include all those who play the game, buy the game, create the game, and make profits from the game. You might even go so far as to include the community surrounding the gamers, such as friends, family, and teachers of game players.

It is neither necessary nor practical to include all stakeholders in all decisions, but it helps to know who they are so you can decide whether they should be given a voice or a vote in decision-making. At a minimum, try to find a way to give at least one representative from each stakeholder group a voice. Some stakeholder groups are so important, they should also be given a vote. A practical approach to inclusive decision-making is to keep in mind this memorable success formula: Everyone gets a voice, but not everyone gets a vote.

You can then further divide your stakeholders into the following subgroups:

DECISION-MAKERS

Decision-makers are the group of people who have the resources, power, and authority to finalize decisions with their votes. Decision-makers should only include those who have the time and energy to fully participate in the process. For this reason, I recommend delegating decisions down to the lowest level possible. Senior leaders often do not have the time to become as informed as they need to be to make a solid decision. Their tight schedules can bottleneck the process.

THOUGHT PARTNERS

When considering which stakeholders to include in the alignment process, it is important to strike a balance. If you keep the group small, it will be more efficient and allow for deeper dialogue. If you keep it too small, you lose the opportunity to include all parties the decision will impact. A nice way to resolve this dilemma is to invite select stakeholders closest to the work to represent each group to serve as Thought Partners during alignment sessions. Thought Partners, unlike decision-makers, do not have a vote, instead, they only have a voice. The primary role of your Thought Partners is to listen and to only intervene if information is missing, including their own perspectives. Thought Partners broaden the perspective in the room and serve as witnesses to support healthy deliberation.

By inviting stakeholders to serve as Thought Partners in your alignment sessions, you allow for a richer diversity of ideas to be shared without bogging down the final decision-making process. Furthermore, when Thought Partners witness the entire decision-making process and have the chance to inform it, they often leave with a better understanding of the rationale behind the decisions made.

TARGETS OF CHANGE

These are people outside of the decision-making group who will need to change their behaviors once the decision is made. For example, if you want to implement a new security system to get into the building, then all employees who need to get into the building are targets of change.

Targets of change are important to identify. When possible, it is best to include them as decision-makers, but, at a minimum, a few should always be included as Thought Partners. For example, recently, I was working with a large technical group in a utility company. The managerial group was in charge of defining the standard operating procedures that the field technicians would use. In this case, the managers were the decision-makers, and the field techs were the targets of change.

We held a two-day alignment session to finalize new standard operating procedures. While the final decision was up to the managers, we invited all the field techs in the session to be Thought Partners, so they could hear the dialogue between the managers and offer their voices to inform decisions. The field techs were allowed to comment and ask questions, but when the time came to finalize the plan, only the managers voted. Prior to this session, the managers had a hard time getting the field techs to comply with procedures; after the session, compliance was much more consistent.

If your alignment process cannot include the targets of change, or at least someone to represent them to serve as Thought Partners, be sure to *roll out,* rather than *throw out* your decision. Don't just email the targets of change new mandates. Instead, have the managers share the decisions that the targets of change must comply with using the 4 Steps of Alignment. This way, managers can spot misconceptions or misalignments before they become a big issue. After completing these sessions, it is worthwhile to reconvene decision-makers if the targets of change are extremely discontented.

SPONSORS

A sponsor is a high-level person who has formal authority over everyone participating in the project. The sponsor must have the authority to hire, fire, promote, and reward everyone on the project. The sponsor could be the company's CEO, or the head of a department, or the manager of a team depending on the span of the group making the decision. If you want to achieve alignment beyond your scope of authority and control, your best first step is to find a sponsor. If you don't have one, tread lightly, as you will only be able to achieve alignment by getting to concordance (everyone agrees 100 percent).

DECIDING WHO TO INCLUDE

The ideal size of the group to include in your alignment sessions will vary by situation. There is a natural tendency to want to keep the circle of people small to speed things up. While aligning more people takes longer, including more people up front pays off in the long run. By including others, you build in added stability and advocacy for the solutions you create together. Most importantly, including more people allows for more diversity.

Increasing diversity in any group is just good business. The more diverse the group, the more likely you are to become aware of something significant to which you might be blind. Diversity also ensures that your chosen solution appeals to and serves the widest possible audience. It's always smart to invite influential people who span different parts of the organization and stakeholder groups. However, once you've done that, the group may still be monolithic. If you don't consider other demographical dimensions of diversity, you may marginalize or disenfranchise underrepresented groups and minorities.

Here are key demographic factors to consider when working to maximize the diversity of the group: race, gender, ethnicity, socioeconomic background, geographic/academic/professional background, personality type, religious beliefs, political beliefs, sexual orientation, heritage, and life experience. Obviously, it's not feasible to include every dimension of diversity every time, but you can always be on the lookout for opportunities to be inclusive. While this might feel daunting, it is a hallmark of courageous leadership and a business best practice with many rewards. After all, *diversity is a fact; inclusion is an act*.

A key advantage of using the 4 Steps of Alignment is that everyone involved must wrestle with views in conflict with their own. This allows each participant to fully understand the implications of the path the group chooses. Those not included in that original wrestling match will have to wrestle with decisions later, and with much less context. The greater the number of stakeholders you include in the alignment process, the less time you will have to spend later selling the decision(s) to stakeholders who weren't included.

You may be tempted to only include fans of your ideas in your deliberations. This can appear to speed up agreement. However, you run the risk that the foes you have not included will feel "dissed" and will lobby against you even when they agree in principle with the agreement reached. The best approach with those you might view as foes is to take the advice of Michael Corleone, as he said in *The Godfather Part II*, "Keep your friends close and your enemies closer." Those you see as foes can help you avoid blind spots caused by groupthink. All stakeholders, across the spectrum from foes to fans, deserve attention. Without the full engagement of them all, you will not achieve true alignment.

If you invite foes to be a part of the decision-making process, be sure to plan for longer sessions to give you time to reconcile dissenting views. If you choose this strategy, you will need to manage your frustration and ego. The first step to effectively work with those who are likely to dissent from your preferred viewpoint is to reframe your view of them. Rather than think of them as foes, think of them in two categories: "canaries in the coal mine" and "demented mentors."

The "canaries in the coal mine" are the people who are extra sensitive to risk. Back in the early days of underground coal mining, the miners would carry a birdcage with a canary and keep it close. The canary was very sensitive to toxic gases that humans wouldn't detect until it was too late. When the mine began leaking gas, the canary would get sick, signaling danger to the miners. Just as no miner would ever dismiss his canary for being too sensitive, you shouldn't ignore the quips of sensitive stakeholders who are more risk-averse than you. If you think of these people as helpful beacons of potential risks, it can be easier for you to accept and value their participation. If you work to provide them psychological safety, rather than dismissing them as "nervous nellies," the quality of your decisions will dramatically improve.

Demented mentors are the people who actively and aggressively challenge your point of view. These people can drive you crazy, but they can also teach you how to be more politically savvy. Listening intently to your demented mentors while managing your ego will help you hear the value they have to offer and eventually get them participating positively. When they realize that you aren't there to fight them, but to understand them, they often become some of the strongest advocates of your decisions.

I like to say, "Judgment divides; inquiry connects." The best way to handle demented mentors is to ask a lot of questions, so they feel thoroughly heard. Also, be sure to highlight areas of alignment and misalignment respectfully. When you detect misalignment, try to accommodate their concerns or voice a rationale for why your preferred solution should move forward. When done skillfully, you will see greater trust in your intentions, both among demented mentors and among those who see you allowing for and embracing dissenting views.

SECTION 4. MEMORABLE SUCCESS FORMULAS

- Everyone gets a voice, but not everyone gets a vote.
- Diversity is a fact; inclusion is an act.
- Always include fans and foes (e.g., canaries and demented mentors).
- Keep your friends close and your enemies closer.
- Judgment divides; inquiry connects.

SECTION 5

HOW TO RUN ALIGNMENT MEETINGS

In this section, we'll discuss the nuts and bolts of running alignment meetings, including logistics, assigning roles, issuing the invitations, and opening the session.

CHAPTER 12

MEETING LOGISTICS

The line between disorder and order lies in logistics.

—SUN TZU

TIME

When it comes to planning alignment meetings, it is valuable to follow the Principle of Versatility by balancing masculine and feminine energies. To run a meeting in a versatile way, use this MSF —*design tight and hang loose*. For example, plan out an agenda to the minute and bring a timer to reinforce it, but also plan for time to let the conversation roll when needed.

Running a meeting in a versatile way makes it harder to predict exactly how much time you need. It depends on the scope of the problem you are trying to solve and the size of the group assembled. A good formula to allow sufficient time for each of the 4 Steps of Alignment is: 20 percent Propose, 60 percent Probe, 10 percent Re-propose, and 10 percent Close. This assumes that a solid re-proposal can be formulated on a break between the second and third steps.

Once you figure out how much time you need for the 4 Steps, add 50 percent. That 50 percent is to provide the slack needed to accommodate the more feminine, emergent parts of the meeting, such as introductions, stretch breaks, late arrivals, connecting activities, and the inevitable twists and turns of emergent feelings.

Creativity is crushed when rushed, and all humans need a little time to process ideas. For every ninety minutes, you need at least a ten-minute break. For meetings longer than half a day, keep the energy flowing by incorporating movement, snacks, and fun activities. For example, I worked with Venkat, a VP who shared a one-minute, funny YouTube video at each meeting; another asked his staff to do high fives with each other whenever good news was shared.

When meetings span several days, I often ask for volunteers to lead a three- to five-minute "art moment," e.g., joke-telling, poetry, rap, or a sing-along. As you can imagine, these requests are usually met with active resistance. However, no matter how good or bad the art moment turns out, it always sparks up the energy. While adding fun takes time, don't skip it—EVER. You will be amazed at how much adding fun enhances creative thinking and improves your odds of success.

SPACE

The space you set up can make a huge difference. Ideally, I set up meetings with round tables or with tables in a U-formation to support interaction between participants. Meetings held around large conference tables make interaction difficult, so only do this if you have no other options.

Sessions conducted in-person are always preferred, but often it is too expensive or just not practical for everyone to be present. Lately, there have been many amazing innovations in virtual technology that allow for teams to interact using video and teleconferencing tools, such as Zoom, Skype, WebEx, and GoToMeeting. These systems are surprisingly affordable and provide both video and audio connections for participants as long as each participant has a computer, a webcam, and a microphone. Video conferencing also has wonderful features like screen sharing, whiteboarding, polling, chat, and recording. Some video conferencing software includes the ability to send participants into smaller groups called breakout rooms. This can make your video conference livelier because more participants can take an active role at the same time. It takes a little practice to master video conferencing, but this is a skill worth acquiring.

Because people are tempted to multitask while attending virtual meetings, it is imperative to establish guidelines for conscious connection such as leaning into the camera, staying fully present, and minimizing distractions by shutting down other programs.

EQUIPMENT

Alignment sessions require minimal equipment; however, the following supplies are helpful to have on hand:

- Handouts
- Notepads and pencils
- Flip charts and markers
- Projection system
- Stickies or index cards
- Tape
- Bell or gong
- Timer
- Snacks

CHAPTER 13

MEETING ROLES

In dreams begin responsibilities.

—WILLIAM BUTLER YEATS

If your meeting includes more than six people, it is very helpful to assign roles. Not only does doing so take the load off of you, it provides an opportunity for others to be more engaged and active in the meeting.

LEADER

The leader is the person in charge of the alignment process. The role of the leader is to set the agenda for the discussion, invite the right players, and set the tone of the meeting. Generally speaking, leaders always have a vote in decision-making; however, sometimes, it is helpful if the leader abdicates his vote to avoid swaying the group too much. Usually, the leader will need to contribute to the content of the discussion. When this is the case, it is best for the leader to go last so that their opinion does not excessively influence the group.

FACILITATOR

The role of the facilitator is ONLY to mind the process. A good facilitator helps provide psychological safety and makes sure that no one is marginalized. For this reason, the facilitator should not be given a voice or a vote. Every meeting needs a facilitator. The leader can serve as a facilitator; however, they must be mindful not to let their interest in the topic at hand distract them from minding the process. If the topic is high stakes, it is best to hire a professional facilitator who is skilled and completely neutral. Hiring a facilitator separates the process from the content and ensures that someone always minds the process. If you can't afford to do so, rotate the facilitator role among the group members.

SCRIBE

As the process unfolds, it is very important to have a scribe keep track of the conversation. Ideally, the scribe makes notes visible by flip charting or projecting notes on a monitor for participants to see. If that isn't possible, a simple note pad will also do the trick. Serving as a scribe can be taxing. Most people cannot scribe effectively for more than two hours, so it helps to rotate the role. Try asking the poorest listener to be the first scribe: the role often enhances his or her listening skills.

It can be helpful to ask the scribe to share the highlights of the conversation with the group rather than just sharing a data dump of their notes. It is customary to give scribes a voice or vote depending on whether they are group members and/or decision-makers.

TIMEKEEPER

Sometimes setting a time limit for discussion is helpful. Rotating the role of timekeeper helps everyone be more conscious of time. However, when I don't have a timekeeper, I like to use an app to keep track of time. My favorite is a free, large-display countdown timer app called Performance Timer. Performance Timer does not sound an alarm when the time runs out. Instead, the numbers turn red, and the timer starts counting up so that you can see how long you've gone over your targeted time.

It is customary to give timekeepers a voice or vote depending on whether they are group members or decision-makers.

CHAPTER 14

ISSUING THE INVITATION

"Transformation occurs through choice, not mandate. Invitation is the call to create an alternative future."

—PETER BLOCK

Now that you have initial considerations and logistics worked out, you are ready to issue invitations to alignment sessions. A well-worded invitation can help set expectations for participants and get their idea machines up and running before they arrive.

Below is an example of what you might include in an email invitation:

> Dear Jules,
>
> We have never really developed a clear strategy for launching our new AI platform. This has led to some conflicts between product management and marketing. Willson has asked me to work up a clear action plan to help the product and marketing teams get on the same page.
>
> Over the next two weeks, I'll be hosting three, two-hour sessions to do that.
>
> Wednesday 5/15 1-3 pm, Wednesday 5/22 1-3 pm and Friday 5/24 1-3 pm in the Mt. Princeton Conference Room.
>
> As head of marketing, your participation is critical. I would very much appreciate your participation in these sessions. However, if you can't attend, please send a suitable delegate. I'll also be inviting Raymond, Jacky, and

Bill. Let me know if you think I should include others. I'd like to keep the session small, so we have time for dialogue, but I also want to make sure I'm not excluding anyone that we need present as we come up with a solid plan that works well across all parts of the organization.

To get things kicked off, I've roughed out an initial proposal (attached). Please consider the proposal as just a starting point, as in our session, we will use a 4 Step process to engage everyone in productive dialogue around this proposal until we are all in agreement.

I look forward to working with you and the rest.

My best,

Moving Up Marvin

CHAPTER 15

THE OPENING

"Do little things as if they were big, so you can do big things as if they were small."

—DOC MITTLEMAN

A good alignment session starts with a strong opening. Take time when you open a meeting to orient everyone so that they know where the meeting is going and can fully participate.

3 PS AND A Q

I recommend the following 3 Ps and a Q formula to open a meeting:

PURPOSE	Clarify the purpose of the meeting.
PAST	Clarify anything that may have transpired prior to the meeting that the participants need to know. This is also a good time to define stakeholders and constraints.
PROCESS	Review the agenda and any processes you may use, such as the 4 Steps, 5 Cs and ground rules.
QUESTION	Confirm that the participants are ready to start and are in agreement about what will be covered and how the meeting will proceed.

PURPOSE

Too often, we start a meeting with no clarity on why we have been convened. Always start by clarifying the purpose of the meeting. This can be as simple as a statement like:

> "I've called the meeting today for us to align on a strategic plan for the next fiscal year."

It can be helpful to further clarify the details of the purpose. For example:

> "If we have a strategic plan in place, we will be able to make more proactive, long-term decisions and be less reactive; the plan should also help us make the best use of our resources."

PAST

Next, you want to briefly review recent events to help participants understand the meeting's context so they all begin at the same starting point.

The Past portion of your opening should answer the following:

- What meetings preceded this meeting?
- What decisions have already been made?
- What step are you on with respect to making the decision currently up for discussion?
- Any current challenges or constraints of which everyone should be aware?
- Which key stakeholders are not attending, and why?

Example of Past statement:

"Prior to this meeting, I met with the board to clarify what authority we have to develop the strategic plan. The board says they totally trust the process and will back up whatever we come up with as long as the strategy does not require structural changes. As you know, we've recently restructured, and the president feels that the organization is worn-out from that and needs a break. Board members will not be attending because they want to give us lots of room to explore our own ideas."

PROCESS

The next step in your opening is to clarify the process you will use to run the session. If you are using the 4 Steps for the first time, it can be helpful to provide the Art of Alignment cheat sheet found in the Appendix to familiarize the group with the 4 Steps and 5 Cs.

Here is an example of how you might orient the group to use the 4 Steps in the meeting:

"In this meeting, we will use a process called the 4-Step Alignment Process. The 4 Steps of Alignment are Propose, Probe, Re-Propose, and Close. More detail is provided in the agenda. The key thing to know: Leslie will present the initial proposal without interruptions. Then, we will use the alignment process to provide feedback. Before the end of the day, we will take a one-hour break so Leslie and I can revise the proposal based on the discussion, and then reconvene in the afternoon to review the changes and finalize our decision."

If the deliberations are complex, be sure to also clarify roles, voices, and votes, the level of agreement, and any constraints. For example:

"We have invited many stakeholders to this session. Everyone in the room will be invited to share their voice about all matters; however, after the deliberation, only the senior leaders will vote on the final decision. The decision will be finalized when all decision-makers have reached consensus. We strive to reach a consensus by tomorrow at 3 p.m. However, if we don't, Leslie and I will make the final call so that we have a strategic

> plan in place by Friday to review at the Monday board meeting. Please keep in mind that we have one constraint: the structure cannot be changed. Otherwise, all options are open for consideration."

Next, lay out the 3 Ps—Purpose, Past, and Process. Once that's done, you have set context for the meeting, and all that's left to do is to add the Q. The Q is a question that invites participants to confirm that they are ready to start.

To add the Q, just ask the audience:

> "How does that sound? Any questions or suggestions for changes?"

Take this question and the responses seriously. Sometimes you may find that you've missed a critical point that will help set the stage for the meeting. Plan for something to come up and to make minor modifications to the agenda on the fly. By adding the Q to your opening, you model the co-creative principle right out of the gate. You also get confirmation that everyone is prepared to start the process in a focused and informed way.

CHAPTER 16

GROUND RULES FOR ALIGNMENT

"Good fences make good neighbors."

—ROBERT FROST

Ground rules are recommended for any meeting, but they are particularly useful when you are dealing with critical decisions. The following meeting ground rules, when followed, will go a long way toward creating psychological safety and the best conditions for alignment.

1. Balance participation.
2. There are no bad ideas.
3. Say what you mean, just don't say it mean.
4. Honor confidentiality.

RULE 1. BALANCE PARTICIPATION

In any meeting, make sure that no one dominates or hijacks the session, and all are contributing in equal measure. To make sure this happens, set equal participation as a ground rule and make sure the facilitation process aligns with it.

One challenge to balancing participation in a large group is the fact that people move at different speeds. Extroverts tend to express their views, while introverts tend to withhold them. Some people have an immediate gut reaction and can think on their feet, while others need more time to feel and think things over. We also tend to think of extroverts and quicker processors as being more energetic or "on the ball" and may give their contributions more weight. Likewise, we often assume that the introverts have nothing to offer, and that people who need time to process information are slow. This is a huge mistake that excludes introverts who have much to offer. Often it is the introverts who are taking in enough information to integrate ideas and see the big picture. Introverts are often thoughtful about when to interject and are just waiting to be asked to offer their insights.

If you aren't careful, the extroverts and quicker processors will dominate the group. If this dynamic is left unchecked, you, as the leader, have marginalized the introverts and those who process ideas more carefully. Even if you have done this unintentionally, you will not reach true alignment without balanced participation.

In a large group, it can be difficult to make sure participation is even. There are many techniques to maximize the number of voices in the conversation. In particular, I like to break large groups into smaller groups then ask for a representative to share the views of the small group. Since the small groups convene at the same time, this allows more people to express themselves. If you are leading a virtual meeting (e.g., Zoom or Skype), you can give everyone a chance to contribute using the chat feature, then discuss the ideas starting with the most frequent theme shared.

RULE 2. THERE ARE NO BAD IDEAS

One fear at play in any group is that of appearing foolish. Often people with great ideas withhold them because they worry they haven't thought them out enough. In reality, half-baked ideas are better than fully baked ideas because they are easier to build upon. People also fear they might say something that isn't accurate and get caught flat-footed.

If the team dynamic is adversarial, people catch each other's mistakes and use them as opportunities to get a leg up on each other. In a psychologically safe environment, we also catch each other's mistakes. However, instead of pointing to the error, we kindly offer additional information to illuminate the topic at hand. When we discover we've made a mistake on a non-adversarial team, rather than feel shame or loss, we feel happy that our colleague helped us clear up misconceptions.

You can create a "safe-to-say," non-adversarial force field that invites all ideas by stating the ground rule that "there are no bad ideas" and then support that statement with your actions. By inviting all ideas, even "bad" or "wrong" ones, you make it safe for people to freely share ideas that haven't been exhaustively researched, and you let the group do the refinement.

RULE 3. SAY WHAT YOU MEAN, JUST DON'T SAY IT MEAN

It is vital to encourage everyone to share their ideas freely and frankly. That said, ask all to speak their mind with kindness. I like to set that up by setting the ground rule:

"Say what you mean, just don't say it mean."

This phrase pretty much sums up everything you need to know about how thoughts should be shared. While we all intend to be kind, sometimes people are unaware that their sharing sounds aggressive.

I once supported a school board as a facilitator. When I started, I noticed that one of the board members, Saul, tended to dominate the meetings. Saul always came prepared. He was a wicked smart guy. As a strategic thinker, he was always challenging the group to think before starting new initiatives. He was also an alpha type, tall and burly with a commanding grizzly bear presence. At one meeting, a proposal was made to launch a new capital campaign. Saul was strongly opposed to the idea. Right after the proposal was presented, Saul leaned forward, raised his voice, and said: "Anyone with half a brain knows it's stupid to ask donors for more money right now." He then literally pounded the table with his fist to underscore his conviction.

As you can imagine, the rest of the board members just sat there in stunned silence. Even if Saul was correct, his aggressive style of communication just sucked the air out of the room. So, I intervened and said, "Saul, your opinion matters, as does that of everyone here. Could you please restate your point of view in a manner that might be easier to hear?" Saul thought for a minute and then said, "I believe that our donors aren't in a position to be generous since we are in the middle of a recession." I then asked if others had a different point of view, and a few then shared the other side of the argument. In the end, they opted to put the campaign on hold for another quarter. This one intervention helped all the board members learn that using shaming and blaming language to express your point of view never helps. Saul was a much better board member after that, and the whole team became more engaged. Generally, asking someone to reframe their statements helps the sender be more thoughtful about their word choice and their impact on others. Had I shamed Saul in the meeting, I would have reinforced the very aggressive and mean behavior that I wanted to stop.

RULE 4. HONOR CONFIDENTIALITY

If the topic being discussed is sensitive or could be misinterpreted by those outside the group, it is important to agree on confidentiality boundaries. Sometimes to create safety in the group, you need to set a very tight boundary. Be sure to set a ground rule that clarifies the boundaries of confidentiality early in the process. If you find the ground rule has been breached, find out why and reestablish a new rule that makes sense for the situation at hand. Remember the famous Vegas tourism slogan, "What happens in Vegas, stays in Vegas?" You can use a similar slogan to remind people to hold tight boundaries around sensitive conversations: "What happens in the room stays in the room."

If the group is speaking about someone not present, be sure that what is said aloud about that person sounds much like what would be said if they were present. This serves to protect every person's dignity and will go a long way toward establishing trust in you and the groups you convene.

SECTION 5. MEMORABLE SUCCESS FORMULAS

- Start meetings with 3 Ps (purpose, past, and process) and a Q
- 4 Ground Rules:

1. Balance participation
2. There are no bad ideas
3. Say what you mean, just don't say it mean
4. What happens in the room, stays in the room

SECTION 6

3D ALIGNMENT

"The key to successful leadership is influence, not authority."
—KEN BLANCHARD

You don't need to have formal power or authority to achieve alignment; however, it is crucial to always respect the lines of authority that exist. If you don't, you may end up in a political quagmire.

We may try to avoid dealing with lines of authority by doing things unilaterally. As they say, "Sometimes it is better to ask for forgiveness than permission." While any decision may be better than no decision, making decisions in a vacuum is bad business. Decisions made unilaterally lead to functional silos and organizational misalignment. For this reason, this part of the book will help you think through how to handle the political forces that vary based on where you fit in the ecosystem. No matter your position in an organization, at some point, you will need to align stakeholders in three directions.

- Bottom-Up: upper management, investors, donors, and board members
- Top-Down: direct reports and vendors
- Sideways: partners, team members, and peers

Each direction requires its own form of political finesse.

CHAPTER 17

TOP-DOWN ALIGNMENT

"Authority is not a power; it is a responsibility."

—AMIT KALANTRI

Alignment in a multilayered organization is always challenging. Conventional wisdom says to start at the top, then cascade decisions down to every level. A Top-Down approach to alignment has many advantages.

- Those at the top have the best vantage point to reconcile competing options and make best use of limited resources.
- Those at the top have the formal authority to make changes.
- Those at the top hold the power of the purse needed to provide incentives.

When changes from the top are effectively managed, it usually leads to alignment.

If you are in a position of authority, you can drive decisions down through the chain of command. As is often said, "When in charge, be in charge." That said, working from the top down has many risks. Messages cascaded down often end up like the messages in a game of telephone. The message of "Don't throw away recycling" gets heard by the last person down the chain as "Don't stop griping."

Furthermore, when senior leaders formulate plans without consulting the targets of change, they often create senseless mandates that have unintended negative consequences.

For example, I worked with one CEO, Oscar, who was frustrated that his company's hiring process was so slow. All departments were running chronically short-staffed. Hiring took so long, that often by the time they made an offer, the candidate had already been snatched up.

Swift to solve the problem, Oscar mandated that HR attend every job interview. Despite his good intentions, this created many problems. Hiring managers complained that having HR present in the interview made them look like they needed a babysitter. With so many interviewers involved, the interview shifted from a casual conversation to a formal process that felt like a dog and pony show. Scheduling interviews among so many people became a logistical nightmare. By the time the interview was finally scheduled, the candidate was long gone.

Ironically, when asked, not even HR was sure why they had to be present in every interview, but they felt they shouldn't challenge the CEO. They assumed that the mandate was implemented because Oscar thought that HR was incompetent. As in a game of telephone, the original message was totally garbled.

Unfortunately, this example of Top-Down alignment by mandate is not unusual. This scenario occurs every day in many organizations, resulting in wasted time, unnecessary expense, and feelings of disempowerment. Over time, those in charge lose the trust of those they lead.

The key to avoiding this dynamic is to make sure that you co-creatively include those closest to the work as Thought Partners and decision-makers. This doesn't mean you have to relinquish your authority. You can always reserve the right to override delegated decisions or feedback from your Thought Partners. Still, by inviting more people to be Thought Partners, you can make your plans well informed and well received by the targets of change.

When Top-Down alignment is done right, you can run your organization more strategically. Most organizations try to do too much, resulting in burnout, dropped balls, and overwhelmed workers. By fostering alignment around a tight strategy, you create focus across the organization.

My client Julie was the managing director of a medical services company. When I started working with her, it seemed like she was holding up the world. She was sure that she had to keep track of all the details to make sure everything ran smoothly. As the business grew, she became the "chief bottlenecker" as she did not have the bandwidth to keep all the balls in the air.

My partner Jen and I finally convinced Julie to focus on a limited number of strategic priorities, then work with all department heads to align their plans around them. It soon became clear that a major issue was tension between operations, which was led by Julie, and sales, which was run by Julie's colleague, Leslie. This tension is common in most companies as sales often promise potential clients things that operations are not prepared to deliver. As a result, quality slips, employees burn out, and frustrations run high.

The solution was obvious: Julie and Leslie needed alignment across the Ops/Sales boundary and all support functions, including Quality, HR, IT, and Finance. We started by holding a retreat with Julie and Leslie. We challenged the two leaders to use the Power of 3s rule to come up with three strategic objectives and three fundamental values that would transform the business unit into a high-performing organization over the next three years. We called it their Transformational Strategic Vision (TSV).

Soon afterward, Julie and Leslie invited the heads of all the other departments to an off-site meeting to review their proposed TSV. The department heads provided rich feedback using the 4 Steps. By the end of the off-site, all department heads had aligned around an improved version of the TSV at a level four or higher. You could see the whole team's energy rise!

Julie and Leslie then asked the department heads to go back to their teams and come up with an action plan to clarify what each department would do to meet the strategic priorities of the TSV.

A month later, they held another retreat with all the department heads to complete the first two steps of the alignment process, Propose and Probe. The intent of the retreat was to allow all the department heads to provide 5 Cs feedback on each other's action plans. We then took a daylong break to allow each department head to formulate a re-proposal based on the feedback received.

Finally, all reconvened to complete the last two steps of the alignment process (Re-propose and Close). The outcome was a focused, three-year strategy for the business unit, and an integrated plan for each department to deliver on the goals. For the first time ever, everyone understood the whole business enough to work in a strategic and coordinated way.

The first year this cascading process was put in place, there was quite a struggle over power and territory. But by the second year, a friendly competition had emerged among the departments. Each leader was eager to show off the marvelous plans they had built with their teams. By the third year, the business unit's performance had moved to the top quartile of the company.

I also saw a big shift in the dynamic between Julie and Leslie. They had always been supportive of each other, but now they were strategic partners working together cohesively. Both became excellent leaders who trusted their teams enough to let go of details and focus on the bigger picture.

Over five years, that business unit went from having a high rate of employee attrition to being voted one of the top ten places to work in Colorado.

Here is the impact of that program in Julie's own words:

"Real results are seen by all of us. I know the members of my staff perform at higher levels, particularly in the areas of focus and accountability. They are further ahead in executing their initiatives than they have been in the past. Our team functions together with much more collaboration than ever before. This change is all due to our off-site sessions and the better understanding we now have of each other and our alignment around goals and objectives."

You also need thoughtful Top-Down alignment when you are delegating. For example, I have weekly staff meetings at which each team member shares the top three tasks they will focus on that week and we use the 4 Steps to align everyone's work. These mini-alignment sessions help us stay focused and get the guidance we need to coordinate our work.

When you are at the top, it can be tempting to tell others what to do, especially if you want them to do things they may not want to do. Forcing should only be a last resort. My client, Docia, was the president of a large insurance company. Docia wanted to promote one of her employees, Helen, to run the claims division. To Docia's surprise, Helen refused to be moved to claims and declined the promotion. Docia was at a total loss. Why would Helen not want to move to claims?

At first, Docia called HR for advice. Genny, the HR rep, advised Docia, "Tell Helen that she has to move. After all, no one in the company gets to choose whom to report to." Docia didn't like the idea of telling Helen to just "Shut up and row," so she asked for a second opinion at our next coaching session. I told Docia it was true; she did have the right to make Helen move, but before doing that, she should give Helen some SHUVA and use the 4 Steps to see if they could align around the move. I told Docia to be prepared; issues might be revealed that she would have to deal with. I also reminded her to use a versatile approach that would uncover not only the facts of the matter but also the feelings that were causing Helen to resist the change.

Here's the email Docia sent soon after her meeting with Helen:

> "Quick update: We were able to successfully navigate the change process. Helen felt the SHUVA and is excited to embrace the new reporting relationship. I learned during our discussion that the real root cause of the uncertainty was the fact that she had reported to Sandra for thirty-one (yes, thirty-one) years. Helen understandably had mixed emotions about leaving that. But she said as she processed the situation, she knew that one way or another, that long working relationship was going to change no matter what. And now, she's excited to work more closely with us toward the company's goals.
>
> Thanks for your help,
>
> Docia"

Docia's story illustrates the power of not forcing alignment, even when you have the right to. If you force change, you risk creating cranky conscripts who spread ill will around them like a virus.

While Top-Down alignment is essential, ideas should always be welcome from every level of the organization, not just the top. By inviting all employees to bring ideas up the chain using the alignment process, you empower your workforce and unleash innovation. Furthermore, your employees should also use alignment practices to ensure any changes they suggest are not disruptive to their peers' work or upper management's future plans.

TOP 3 TIPS FOR TOP-DOWN ALIGNMENT

1. Be aware of your psychological size
2. Delegate
3. Be a good sponsor

BE AWARE OF YOUR PSYCHOLOGICAL SIZE

One simple but critical thing to be mindful of in Top-Down alignment is the concept of "psychological size." You can also refer to this phenomenon as the "Bruce Springsteen Effect." Imagine Bruce giving a concert. Not only is Bruce on stage with thousands of people watching his every move, he is also projected on five big screens twenty feet high. You can see every bead of sweat on The Boss' forehead, every ripple of muscle under his T-shirt. Well, it's the same for you as "The Boss" of your company—people see you in much more detail and at a size much larger than your actual one; they expect so much of you. You see yourself as just a normal human. You probably don't realize that your psychological size has a significant impact on those who report to you.

Because of your psychological size, if you put your ideas out there first, you will stack the deck in favor of your own views and prevent full expression from your team. For that reason, it is always wise for the most senior person in a room to share their views last. Going last will decrease the risk of pandering to win your favor and increase the odds of your team operating as capable Thought Partners.

DELEGATE

By delegating initiatives to those who show leadership potential, you can leverage your time and actively develop your leadership pipeline.

You can use the 4 Steps of Alignment to delegate a project to someone else. Here's how that might look:

Propose

> "Susan, I would love for you to be the lead on a new project. Right now, project management is done in each department separately, leading to 'random acts of project management.' I'd like us to move toward having one project management function that integrates all project management efforts. Since this will touch every department, I think we need input from all departments. I'd like you to invite a rep from each department in creating a plan to centralize the function. I've got this book called *The Art of Alignment* that has a great process you can use to help the group make decisions and arrive at an aligned plan."

Probe

(be sure to take notes!)

You can let Susan know this is not a mandate, but just a suggested plan and that you really want to know what she thinks. Here are how the 5 Cs might play out:

- Clarifications: “Does what I’m proposing make sense?”
- Compliments: “I’m curious. Is this something you would like to do?”
- Concerns: “What concerns do you have about leading this project?”
- Changes: “What would you change about this project if it were entirely up to you?”
- Commitment: “Is this something you are okay doing? If you don’t feel jazzed about it, please say so.”

Re-Propose

Hopefully, you’ve been taking notes on Susan’s reactions. At this stage, either wrap Susan’s ideas into a re-proposal or ask Susan to make the re-proposal.

> “We’ve been talking a while now; would you mind taking a stab at stating where we’ve landed?”

Close

Work with Susan to finalize any next steps and deadlines and ask her to send you a quick email detailing what you and she have discussed and agreed to.

> “Sounds like a plan. Would you mind writing up a quick email to summarize things, so we don’t forget what we discussed? Here are my handwritten scribbles if that helps.”

BE A GOOD SPONSOR

When you delegate projects to someone else, it is crucial to play the role of the sponsor to help set them up for success. This is especially true if the person to whom you've delegated the project doesn't have authority over everyone involved in the project. Most people are happy to be a sponsor; however, they don't know what to do to sponsor a project effectively.

Effective sponsors do the following:

1. Grant visible authority to the project leader
2. Create a compelling rationale for the project
3. Manage competing priorities
4. Keep tabs on the project
5. Give the group freedom
6. Provide resources
7. Provide "top-cover"
8. Create an empowered culture

GRANT VISIBLE AUTHORITY

Make sure to be present at the project launch to pass your mantle of authority to the project leader explicitly. Granting authority could sound like:

"I've asked Susan to lead this project and am grateful she has accepted. Susan will be working with you to get this done by March. I wish I had time to lead it myself. However, I know Susan will do a great job. Please consider her a proxy for me; if you have any challenges with this project, bring them to Susan. She and I will meet weekly to review progress and get you any answers or resources you need."

CREATE A COMPELLING RATIONALE

For every project, be sure to create a compelling rationale for why the change that the project is designed to achieve matters. All change projects should align with your strategy, values, and legal regulations. Your project manager can help you figure out how to articulate the rationale as effectively as possible. Once you have the rationale clear, be sure to use every opportunity to socialize it so that people get why it matters.

Example:

> "This last year, almost every project had significant delays and cost overruns in large part because we didn't have a solid project management process in place. By consolidating project management, we can make sure the highest priority projects get the attention they deserve, and we can apply specialized expertise across multiple regions. If we get this right, we can improve our performance significantly."

MANAGE COMPETING PRIORITIES

All organizations need to evolve and change. However, too many changes at once can overwhelm a system, especially if they aren't well-coordinated and managed. Top-Down alignment must thread the needle so that enough change is happening for the organization to grow, but not so much that you end up with burnout or, even worse, projects that fail because there isn't enough time, money, or energy to make them happen. Bear in mind, when it comes to growing your business, there is *always* an unlimited demand on our time, money, and energy, but there really is a limited supply of these resources. As a person of authority, it is your job to manage priorities strategically by saying yes to some projects and no to others, especially if your employees are overburdened.

Too much change is no joke; in some cases, it can be life-threatening. For example, a hospital I worked with was relocating to a much larger and more technological campus. At the same time, they were also shifting from paper to digital records, all while responding to legislated changes in insurance reimbursements. On top of all that, once they moved to their new location, they needed to double in size quickly to pay for their new facility. While every change was worthwhile and exciting, after about a year, the employees started to look like zombies stumbling around.

Carmen, a department leader I was coaching, was so overcommitted she had a chronic bladder infection because she was too busy to get to the bathroom, much less get to the end of her to-do list. In a hospital environment, being overwhelmed is not just uncomfortable; there is a real risk that someone could die if they don't get the care they need.

As a person at the top, you have to make sure that you are not asking employees to do more than is humanly possible. Otherwise, you are creating an "unfunded mandate," meaning a mandate you aren't providing employees enough resources to fulfill. Unfunded mandates are a recipe for failure. Either the project will stall, or it will drain resources from other vital projects. This is why it is key that you prevent "change overload" by limiting the number of initiatives happening at a given time. If you can't find time to be an engaged and effective sponsor of all the initiatives you have delegated, you are probably in change overload and need to dial it back.

KEEP TABS ON THE PROJECT AND REMOVE BARRIERS AND BOTTLENECKS

Likely your project manager will not have authority over everyone involved in the project. As a person with formal authority, you can remove barriers your project leader might not be able to move. For this reason, be sure to meet with the project manager regularly to keep tabs on how the project is going and how well your direct reports are participating.

If the project manager is struggling to get people to participate, rather than casting blame, work with him or her to troubleshoot and use your power and authority to back the manager. Perhaps the invited group doesn't understand why the project matters. If so, perhaps you should talk about the project at staff meetings or a town hall or add a blurb to your next communication outreach.

Could it be that participants have conflicting priorities that prevent them from participating fully? If so, only you or their boss can resolve that issue. Either way, you need to intervene to make sure priorities are clear and you aren't asking more of your people than they can deliver. If the project starts to slip or fall apart due to poor participation, don't look to blame the project leader or the participants. Instead, look in the mirror. As a person of authority, this is your problem to solve.

GIVE THE GROUP FREEDOM

When you delegate a project, set a few guidelines and criteria for success, then give the group lots of room to arrive at their own solutions. They may come to you asking for guidance or want to run ideas by you to make sure you are really on board. Seeking your concurrence is not a bad practice. However, be mindful that your preferences and opinions may have undue influence and may cramp the group's creativity. After attending the initial meeting and passing the baton to your project leader, step back. Ask more questions. Offer less advice.

PROVIDE RESOURCES

Convening people to work together on cross-organizational projects often requires resources: a professional facilitator, space for convening, web conferencing platforms, audiovisual equipment, computing resources, printing, T-shirts, and swag. Ask your project manager to estimate the resources required. If reasonable, approve the expenditure to adequately fund the project and give them the latitude to manage their own budget.

PROVIDE "TOP-COVER"

Sometimes projects fail; this is just reality. If the project succeeds, always be sure to give your project manager and their Thought Partners credit. However, if the project fails, assume responsibility for the failure. After all, you commissioned the project and should have been involved enough to provide guidance. When you have the courage to own the failure, you model a higher standard of accountability. You will also embolden leaders of future projects as they will know you always have their backs.

CREATE AN EMPOWERED CULTURE

As a person in charge, you are in a position to create a culture of empowerment by actively inviting all to play a role in shaping the future of your company. Set the expectation that even the lowest-level worker, like a janitor or a cafeteria server, can bring forward an idea and get concurrence, up, down, or sideways any time.

An excellent way to do this is to provide training for all employees on alignment principles and practices, so they all share a common language. Be sure to complement this training with a clear process for ideas to be brought forward for consideration and sponsorship.

For example, you could host an annual “Idea Jam,” where employees propose ideas on how to improve the company to senior leaders for serious consideration. When an idea emerges that has promise, be sure it is well sponsored and enthusiastically socialize any wins achieved as a result of it.

A utility company we worked with incorporated an Idea Jam into their leadership development program. Program participants were asked to answer these questions: “What is holding the company back from achieving its full potential, and what ideas do you have to address these challenges?” Many ideas were explored. Some rose to the top while others fell off the table. The participants were then invited to select and refine the best into a few simple proposals to share with Brad, the CEO, using the 4 Steps of Alignment.

As the conversation with Brad deepened, everyone gained clarity on which ideas were ripe and why it might not be the right time to implement some of the good ideas that emerged. Some ideas were such “no brainers” that we wondered why they hadn’t been done already. Brad immediately commissioned leaders from the group to manage two projects and offered to serve as their sponsor.

This Idea Jam not only produced game-changing initiatives; it helped all the emerging leaders feel empowered to bring ideas to the table in the future.

You can greatly improve intrapreneurship and innovation by making the 4 Steps of Alignment a common practice in your organization. By doing so, you will create a culture of empowerment and high engagement.

CHAPTER 18

BOTTOM-UP ALIGNMENT

"One voice can change a room."

—BARACK OBAMA

When you don't have the power or authority to make a change, you may feel it is not your place to even suggest one. I don't believe in that. If you have an idea that can create a better future, then why hold back, even if you are at the very bottom of an organization? You just need the know-how to step outside the lines and the patience to work iteratively to bring others along. If your idea crosses organizational boundaries, you will need finesse, diplomacy, and change management skills.

When a client's vision outstrips their level of authority, I often hear complaints about what other people should do. For example:

- "The managing partner *should* make sure all senior associates have equal access to the help of interns."
- "Upper management *should* address burnout; we are so overworked."
- "We need clear direction; without it, I have no idea how to prioritize my work."

In my work as an executive coach, I am often surprised at how timid even the most senior-level executives can be. Take, for example, one client, Alan, a VP of a software company. Alan complained that his customers were leaving because the latest release of the software was full of bugs, and promised updates were chronically behind schedule. Upon further exploration, he revealed that when issues came up at senior team meetings, there was never any discussion about how to resolve them. It was like the movie *Groundhog Day*. The exact same problems showed up again and again with almost no forward movement.

I asked, “It sounds like you know the issue. What can you do to fix it?” Alan replied with many great ideas. He would create an online dashboard that could be used to flag a few challenges for group discussion. He would then refocus the agenda on troubleshooting the most pressing issues on the dashboard.

So, the rest of the conversation went like this:

“Who runs the meetings?” I asked.

“Laura,” he replied.

“Ok, then, what does Laura think about your idea?” I asked.

“Well, I’ve never discussed it with her,” he replied.

“Why not?” I asked.

“I guess I don’t want to overstep my boundary,” he replied.

I pointed out that he wasn’t overstepping a boundary if the process led by Laura impacted his customers. Not to mention that he wasn’t the only one whose time was being wasted. Furthermore, the senior team meetings included twelve execs, each making hundreds of dollars per hour, so at every meeting, thousands of dollars were being wasted. Even worse, there was a real risk of losing customers, which could cost the company millions. At this point, I challenged Alan by saying, "I am here to serve as your coach to help you be a better leader. If this problem is impacting you, your clients, and your peers, then your leadership can help. It *is* your responsibility to improve the situation, even if you aren't in charge of the meeting."

Alan reluctantly agreed. I then pointed out that Alan could honor the lines of authority by using the 4 Steps of Alignment with Laura to propose meeting improvements that might resolve their issues. Alan did follow my advice and asked Laura for a meeting. He approached her in a deferential manner, asking permission to offer an idea that might improve the meeting. Laura turned out to be quite receptive, as she, too, sensed the meetings were ineffective and was at a loss over what to do.

Many of my clients feel frustrated and powerless because they believe they must only do what their boss asks of them. While there are some bosses out there whom you really can't influence, most love it when their employees proactively come to them with ideas for improvements.

I always encourage my clients to step out of reactivity and into creativity by formulating a proposal to clarify the areas where they need more direction or sponsorship. An example was my work with Claire, the head of training for a software company. Claire was always operating in "firefighter" mode because she didn't have a clear picture of training demands. She basically acted as an order-taker, taking in requests for training and coordinating them until the funds ran out.

In our coaching calls, Claire would complain about the lack of direction from above. I said, "Claire, this is the perfect opportunity for you to lead. If you don't know what to do, just make an educated guess, socialize it, and see if you can get the mystery cleared up. If you wait for your boss to do this for you, you will probably be waiting forever."

She took this advice to heart and reluctantly asked her boss, Karen, for permission to pull together a draft training plan and budget and run it up the chain of command to get approval. To Claire's surprise, Karen was thrilled. Claire started the process by interviewing programmers to find out what technical and soft skills they anticipated needing over the next three to five years. Next, she interviewed the trainers to get a better understanding of what they needed to deliver on the demands of the programmers. With these two perspectives, Claire formulated a proposal that outlined the top priorities, schedule, and budget for training.

Claire used the 4 Steps of Alignment to get feedback on her proposal from programmers and trainers and left the session with an even stronger plan. She then did an alignment session with Susan. Susan was concerned that Claire's proposal might be rejected because the funds requested were so much higher than those requested the year before. Karen suggested Claire make two changes: first, add an ROI calculation to justify the higher spending, and second, draw up a backup proposal that matched last year's spending level.

Claire then prepared a clever presentation to Jonathan, the CEO, showing the full-blown plan first. She clearly explained why each element was needed. On the next slide, she showed the same plan with boxes greyed out, representing what would need to be cut if they stayed with the current funding level. She finished by clarifying that while the full-blown plan was a bigger investment, it clearly delivered a higher ROI than the stripped-down version.

She then used the 4 Steps with Jonathan to confirm the level of spending he was committed to. To everyone's surprise, he decided that the full-blown plan was an excellent investment, given how strategically the money was to be spent. Claire went back to the programmers with the good news. Now, they had assurance that the training they needed would be there.

The next year, she repeated the process and asked for even more support from the CEO. This time, with the backing of the head of programming, she asked to double the training budget to hire more trainers and a training coordinator she would manage. Jonathan approved the higher budget and commended Claire and Karen for being so proactive in getting the training they needed to adapt to disruptive technology changes.

While Claire's story was a big success, I have also had clients who made recommendations that were not approved. If this happens to you, don't consider it a failure. At least you've given the opportunity a shot. Just remember, if you don't ask for what you want, you probably will never get it. If you do ask, you may get it, or you may not. Not only that, a "no" can help you focus your efforts where there is more readiness. If you make asking for what you want a consistent practice, over time, you will get more of what you want.

TOP 3 TIPS FOR BOTTOM-UP ALIGNMENT

1. Create readiness for change
2. Always honor lines of authority
3. Get top-cover

CREATE READINESS FOR CHANGE

Have you ever had a great idea, then found that when you shared it with others, it just fell flat, or worse, people just hated it? This is not unusual. The first time someone hears an idea that changes the current trajectory, they will likely have a critical reaction.

With the 4 Steps of Alignment, you don't need people to agree with your initial proposal right out of the gate. However, you also don't want people to kill the idea before even giving it a chance.

Think of it this way: your ideas are like seeds of corn. If you drop corn onto hard, dry dirt, it is unlikely to sprout. However, if you plow the field first, your corn will grow into a bumper crop. So, if your idea is "out of the box" and shifts the status quo, be sure to plow the field. Socialize your proposal with a few key stakeholders privately before ever discussing it in public.

When people are comfortable with the status quo, they will resist emerging ideas. For this reason, I recommend that you socialize your ideas as much as possible. In a risk-averse environment, it can take someone seven times to hear an idea before they really listen. So, if your idea gets an initial adverse reaction or "no," don't give up. Instead, just repeat the idea a new way and don't overreact when dissenting views show up. Lightly suggest the idea with a qualifier such as "What if..." or "How about..." or "Hey, here's a random idea I just had..." The critical point is to use the language of possibility in an unattached dreamy way.

Don't fight adverse reactions. It can be tempting to try to convince the dissenting person that they are wrong, and you are right. Resist that urge. Instead, just count this as one of the seven times you will need to say something before it is heard or understood. Thank the person for their opinion, be patient, and bring it up again later. Ideally, with each iteration, use something the person brought up in your last call to improve your idea. You might even start referring to it as *their* idea.

By socializing your idea privately, you can prevent dissenters from contaminating each other. Instead of focusing on "no" people, look for "yes" people, and cultivate them. When someone reacts positively, ask that person to back you up the next time you bring the idea up in public. If you aren't the only one in favor of your idea, it won't sound so wild to others in the room.

ALWAYS HONOR LINES OF AUTHORITY

When your ideas reach beyond your area of accountability, honor the chain of command. If your concern falls in someone else's jurisdiction, don't go around them. If you do, you risk ruining a relationship that you might need at some point. Instead, approach them in a respectful and deferential manner. Let them know that you respect their position and do not intend to undermine them. Ask for permission to offer your ideas for their consideration. If they seem open, be sure to position your idea as an alternative course of action. Never imply that your idea is something they should do or should have done already. Once you propose your idea, probe using the 5 Cs.

If they aren't excited about the idea, don't push back too hard. Instead, thank them for listening, and let them know you understand it is up to them to take or leave your ideas. Graciously agree to disagree and do your best to keep the relationship intact. If you succeed in closing with respect, you may find that your suggestion has more impact than was apparent. Remember that it never helps to be in a power struggle with someone who owns the keys to the car you want to drive. Instead, find a way to support that driver from the passenger seat. If they don't permit you to help them, you may need to step out of the car and look for another vehicle. Be sure to preserve the relationship, and over time, you will find that you will have more respect and credibility, and your ability to influence others will increase.

GET TOP-COVER

If your idea requires people who don't report to you to do something new, you need top-cover from someone senior to you. Don't wait for someone to take you under their wing. Instead, proactively recruit a mentor or a sponsor. I tell all my clients to identify senior leaders they admire and ask them to be mentors. Your mentor can play a key role in helping you think through how to position a proposal or deal with sticky challenges that may come up.

Many companies have formal mentoring programs. If yours does, take advantage of it. If not, you don't need a matchmaker to find a mentor. All you really need to do is ask. Nine times out of ten people are flattered and impressed with the initiative of the person requesting mentorship. Once your mentor has agreed, take the lead in setting up informal meetings to get to know each other and establish trust. That way, when you hit a bump in the road, you have someone you can go to who can provide advice, coaching, and a reality check.

For example, I coached Paul, an IT director in an aerospace company, to find a few senior leaders to mentor him. Paul stepped up to the challenge and set up regular meetings with several mentors. Not long after, Paul's team was told they had to move to offices far from the system they managed. This meant that every time the system went down, it would take his team twice as long to bring it back online. I asked Paul if any of his mentors could provide advice. Immediately he thought of Mitzi, the CIO, who would surely have some idea how he might get the decision reversed. Fortunately, Mitzi was more than happy to offer Paul advice on how to make his request. Mitzi also offered to step in if the request for reconsideration had any political fallout. Paul was then able to more confidently make his case, and he got the decision reversed.

Sometimes having a mentor is not enough. If you are running a project that requires the involvement of people who do not report to you, you need a sponsor who holds authority over all players involved. If you haven't been assigned a sponsor, enroll one. Be sure to read chapter 17 on Top-Down Alignment to get a clear picture of what a good sponsor does. Whether you are assigned a sponsor or have to recruit one, ask them to read chapter 17 too. Then meet to discuss whether they are willing to engage in the sponsoring behaviors listed. If they seem reluctant to engage in some or all of the eight behaviors of effective sponsors, you are taking on a no-win situation. Either the organization isn't ready, or you are in an unfunded mandate. Rather than pushing forward, try to gracefully bow out or postpone the project, and go back to plowing the field until there is more readiness for change.

CHAPTER 19

SIDEWAYS ALIGNMENT

"Coming together is a beginning, staying together is progress, and working together is success."

—HENRY FORD

Sometimes you need alignment in a system where there is no power differential. Examples include partners in a business, working in a coalition of peers, or working with volunteers where no one is in charge. Every once in a while, I work with teams and organizations that have no hierarchy because they value equity so much that every person has an equal vote. In these cases, alignment principles and practices can keep things moving forward.

One example was a team of three co-founders I coached. They created a holistic approach to funerals that breaks away from the traditional model of a funeral home. They offered affordable and environmentally friendly personalized options for cremations and burials.

Mercedes acknowledged that despite being "amazing partners," she and her co-founders, Aiko and Oliver, were struggling to get the business up and running. They were having difficulty making the decisions needed to prepare to open the doors to the business. Several areas of misalignment had cropped up. Challenges threatened progress, and they were on the verge of giving up on their dream. This is not uncommon in founder groups when the founders have various levels of risk—one may have put in more money, another more time, and yet another may have more subject matter expertise. This diversity of gifts creates a strong co-founder team but increases the risk of misalignment and stalls decision-making.

So, I spent a few hours with the three co-founders and taught them the 4 Steps of Alignment. We identified three areas around which they needed to align: 1) the budget, 2) closing the funding gap, and 3) a plan for the opening of their first funeral home. The three co-founders were each assigned the task of coming up with a proposal to run by the other two. A week later, we reconvened for two hours. In that session, Mercedes, Aiko, and Oliver reached alignment on the budget and left so excited about the breakthrough that they went off to lunch and worked through the other two areas.

They later informed me that that day was instrumental in them becoming secure enough to stick it out. The process not only allowed them to get the budget, funding, and project plan in place, it also helped them blow through challenges that came up when they finally opened the doors to their new funeral home.

Usually, sideways alignment is needed in small groups sharing power, but it can also work in a larger system that values collaboration. I was hired by a private school to help them create HR policies that aligned with their principles and the labor laws of the state. This particular institution operated differently from most. Typically, the board and administration make all the policies, but in this school, the teachers play an equal role in running it. The founders believe deeply in using a consensus-based, decision-making model to keep their tight-knit community together. As you can imagine, this means that decisions take a long time.

The school needed a policy to handle teacher performance issues and eventual dismissal if needed. I started by conducting an online survey to ask a few simple questions. What challenges did they face concerning performance issues and termination? What ideas did they have for a better policy?

After consulting state labor regulations, I formulated a draft policy from the survey feedback and used the 4 Steps to get feedback from the director, the board chair, and a few teachers on key committees.

Next, we held an all-hands session with forty people, including administrative staff, faculty, and a few board members. At the all-hands session, we divided the group into eight groups of five. We broke the policy down into eight sections and assigned a section to each group. Each group reviewed their section using the 5 Cs then formulated a re-proposal. We then reconvened the full group to review the re-proposals and used Fist to Five polling to reach consensus on every section of the policy. The final result was a policy that everyone embraced. An added benefit was that when the policy was later implemented, both the person with the performance challenge and their manager knew exactly what to expect.

TOP 3 TIPS FOR SIDEWAYS ALIGNMENT

1. Divide and conquer
2. Don't confuse consensus with concordance
3. Use a neutral facilitator

DIVIDE AND CONQUER

For groups where the power is dead-even, it can be tempting to try to get everyone in a room to come up with an initial proposal. This is generally not the best use of anyone's time. Instead, ask for a volunteer or two to work up a proposal offline and bring it back to the group for an alignment session. A pre-formulated proposal will give the group something concrete to react to and help the group shift from divergent to convergent conversations for committed action.

NEVER CONFUSE CONSENSUS WITH CONCORDANCE

Often when working within a group of equals, it can be tempting to keep the conversation going until everyone is happy. Many confuse consensus (when participants are satisfied enough with the plan that they can stand behind it) with concordance (when all participants are totally satisfied with the plan). Keep in mind that while reaching concordance is ideal, consensus is usually good enough. Generally speaking, achieving concordance just isn't worth the extra time and energy it takes.

Before going into a decision, clarify the level of agreement you are seeking. If you want to reach for concordance, go for it. However, if you get stuck, ask the group if it will accept a consensus or democratic decision instead. Remind the group of these distinctions along the way and test for commitment often to make the level of agreement transparent. This can help the group avoid an endless debate about minor details that don't really matter.

USE A NEUTRAL FACILITATOR

Often, groups with even power don't want any given member of the group to be the leader. If this is the case, get an external facilitator. Have the facilitator put a process in place to elicit volunteers to draft up proposals for the group to consider. Provide a template and tools for the proposals so that the people drafting them are clear on the level of detail needed. Be sure to remind them not to feel too much pressure to craft the perfect proposal, as the whole group will help them improve upon their ideas.

SECTION 6. MEMORABLE SUCCESS FORMULAS

- Be aware of your psychological size
- Don't set up an unfunded mandate
- Plow the field before planting your seeds
- Always honor lines of authority
- Always get top-cover
- Never confuse consensus with concordance

SECTION 7

TROUBLESHOOTING

"The secret of many a man's success in the world resides in his insight into the moods of men and his tact in dealing with them."
—J. G. HOLLAND

Unfortunately, it only takes one disruptive person to hijack a meeting and throw everything off the rails! If and when disruptive behavior happens, be sure to intervene early, before things escalate.

If discussions keep getting hung up, or people are digging in, double down on the Principles of Alignment. If you provide a lot of SHUVA and psychological safety, you will deescalate conflict, and people are more likely to line up. However, if you ignore people's social and emotional needs, passive-aggressive behaviors will show up.

The bottom line is this: the speed at which you reach alignment is directly proportional to your ability to take care of the social and emotional needs of your stakeholders, decision-makers, and Thought Partners. To do this, pay attention to whom you include in the first place, then actively manage disruptive behaviors swiftly and compassionately. This section explains how to do that.

CHAPTER 20

DEALING WITH DISRUPTORS

"We all have private ails. The troublemakers are they who need public cures for their private ails."

—ERIC HOFFER

When someone interferes with progress, it can be tempting to label them as a troublemaker and dismiss them. Labeling is not helpful, as it blames them for being offtrack and gives you an excuse to do nothing. Rather than thinking of these people as problems, think of them as valuable contributors who are using reactive behaviors to meet their otherwise unmet needs.

According to leadership gurus Bob Anderson and Bill Adams, reactive behaviors tend to fall into three categories: controlling, protecting, and complying. Controllers push their ideas too hard, crowding out others; protectors withdraw to stay safe; and compliers overaccommodate to be accepted. Each of these reactive behaviors is a counterproductive attempt to feel safe in a group. All forms of reactivity undermine the contribution of the reactive person and negatively impact the entire group. As the leader, you can minimize disruption by identifying reactive behaviors and intervening swiftly to help the player get their need met in a healthy way.

Before you address any negative behavior in someone else, start with yourself. Manage your own reactivity, so you don't take out your frustration on your team. While it may seem silly, a few techniques that can help are taking three deep breaths, counting backward, and journaling. Once you have control of your reactivity, you are in a position to help. If you aren't in control of yourself, just wait.

Each person's public reputation is sacred to them. If you reprimand someone in front of the group, you may very well do permanent damage to their credibility. Furthermore, the whole team will witness this, and the psychological safety of the group will be broken. Bear in mind: *fear is inversely proportional to innovation*, so you might as well have just turned off the lights for your team. Handle all troublemaking behaviors gently and kindly with your reactivity in check, and you will go far.

A key rule to keep in mind is, "Never, ever, let anyone lose face in public."

When someone does something that violates a ground rule, rather than reprimand them directly, remind the whole group of the ground rules. Your reminder should not single anyone out and should be said in a friendly tone.

This can be as simple as saying, "It seems like we are wandering away from our ground rules; let's take a pause and read through them quickly to remind ourselves how to show up."

If you find that someone has a disruptive pattern despite these preventative steps, your best strategy is to address the problematic behavior in private. The following list of the top ten most common disruptive behaviors can help you spot reactive patterns, meet unmet needs, and skillfully redirect disruptors.

TOP 10 DISRUPTIVE BEHAVIORS AND WHAT TO DO ABOUT THEM

1. GRANDSTANDERS

Grandstanding is talking dramatically about an idea for much longer than is useful. People grandstand when they are passionately attached to an idea. Often, they have good intentions and suggestions but tend to bring out their ideas too early and overwhelm other participants with their laser-focus. When a grandstander finishes, there is a risk the next person will emulate their behavior. In this situation, redirect the group by calling on the person who has spoken the least. You can also set a time limit on sharing, such as thirty seconds or a minute.

Sometimes the grandstander is not really attached to a concept. Instead, they grandstand because they are attached to the concept being *their* idea. They crave attention and recognition. They may appear to be confident, when in reality, controlling behavior creeps up because they are deeply insecure.

You can appeal to this motivation to be seen and admired by asking the person to clarify their points with you, or you can acknowledge the good points they have already offered. Sometimes this extra dose of attention and validation can help the person to relax. If the grandstander has landed on a helpful idea, be sure to grab that idea and give them credit, so they get a little of what they need.

A tip to help grandstanders is to flip chart their comments, then ask if you've captured them correctly. By taking the extra time to confirm you've "got it," you might finally stop the endless repetition.

2. SIDEWINDERS

Sidewinders take the conversation off track. Often, they bring up things out of order, talk too long about something, or get lost in detail. Unfortunately, if you don't manage them, their lack of discipline can spread like a virus among the group. If you have a sidewinder in the group, an excellent facilitator is worth her weight in gold. But if you can't afford to hire a facilitator, remember that someone must mind the process!

The great thing about using the 4 Steps of Alignment consistently is that once the group knows the steps, they get better at keeping each other on track. Following the 4 Steps and the 5 Cs in order is key to preventing sidewinding behaviors. To manage serious sidewinding, let the group know that to keep them on track, you will be a stickler for following the 4 Steps in order and limit the time for sharing. Your best trick here is to ask each person to write down their thoughts for every line of inquiry you initiate. Writing before speaking will increase intentional expression and focus. Another trick to managing sidewinding is to use hand signals. Let the group know your gesturing is not intended to be rude but is intended to help the group be more efficient without interrupting the discussion.

If you need to handle the sidewinder one-on-one, let her know that time is very tight and that you would appreciate her being more focused and concise. You might even agree to a secret hand signal: such as bringing your two index fingers together to signal it is time to close the conversation.

3. TRAIN WRECKERS

Train wreckers are those who go along in the beginning, but then bring up points late in the discussion that should have been brought up earlier, effectively throwing the "train off the track." By using the 4 Steps consistently, you can teach participants to make sure to express concerns during the Probe step. You can prevent train wrecking by setting a ground rule up front: no one is not allowed to express concerns in the Re-Propose step if their concern was not already voiced during the Probe step.

When train wrecking becomes a habit, perhaps the person knows it gives them the spotlight. In one meeting I facilitated, I noticed that one employee, Alan, had a pattern of waiting to go last and then bringing up something novel or contrary to what had already been shared. After a while, I began to wonder if this was a calculated move to get the group's undivided attention. I asked for a private conversation and asked that he be more mindful of when the timing is right for divergent thinking and when for convergent thinking. This was enough to break Alan's habit.

4. HERMITS

Hermits are quiet participants who tend to sit silently. Frequently, we allow this behavior, believing that if someone has something to share, they will speak up. Never assume that the quiet people have nothing to share. More often than not, the hermits are sitting on great ideas and are astute observers of the group. It is very helpful for you to set the expectation that everyone must contribute and call people out by name to even-out participation in the group.

To help the hermits speak up, I often ask for the person who has spoken least to lead the next point of discussion. On a break, it can be helpful to ask the hermit for his observations to help him feel valued. If you sense that the hermit is upset, it is also helpful to gently check-in to see if this is the case.

5. CONSPIRATORS

Conspirators are politically savvy players who lobby privately before and after alignment sessions to get their needs met. You know you have a conspirator in the mix when every time you reconvene, the tone of the group has shifted, and whatever alignment you have achieved has started to unravel. To manage conspirators, set ground rules up front about what kinds of discussions should happen in the room and out of the room. While your participants are unlikely to follow these rules, just setting them can limit offline conversations that disrupt the alignment process.

If you discover that conspiratorial offline conversations have been happening, you can meet with the conspirators and discuss why they aren't expressing themselves in the meeting. Let them know dissent is welcome. True alignment can only happen if everyone is transparent, even if this slows things down.

6. FLATLINERS

Sometimes you have participants who are just flat-out disinterested and check out. I call this behavior flatlining. Flatliners can suck the energy out of the room. Whenever possible, I recommend making your alignment sessions optional, not mandatory, to avoid forcing flatliners to attend. Flatlining occurs for a number of reasons: people don't feel well, or are close to retirement, or don't feel connected, or don't have a role to play but were invited as a courtesy. Have a private conversation with the flatliner to remind her that her presence matters and see if there is a deeper issue you can help resolve. If not, sometimes it is better to excuse the person than to insist that she participate.

7. GHOSTS

Ghosts are invited participants who don't show up and never say why. Ghosts can set a precedent that it is okay to skip alignment sessions. They can also lead people to think that you had never invited them in the first place. If you have a ghost on your hands, be sure to take the time to check in with them. Confirm that he got the invitation, and if he did, find out why he elected not to come. Ghosting can occur for many reasons, but usually: 1) The ghosts are using their absence as a passive-aggressive protest, 2) They feel that their input is not necessary, or 3) they are busy with more pressing concerns. No matter what the reason, offer SHUVA and let them know not only that their input matters, but why it matters. If they still elect not to participate, ask them to explicitly express the reasons by writing up a statement to share with the group that clarifies their election not to participate and recuse themselves. If they are just too busy to attend, ask that they consider sending a surrogate to represent their views.

8. CURMUDGEONS

Curmudgeons are doubters who feel they have to point out flaws and risks. Having a curmudgeon in your group can feel like having a sandbag in your hot air balloon. Keep in mind that this behavior does serve as a grounding influence to prevent the group from flying off into the stratosphere. Curmudgeons think they are helping by bringing flaws to the group's attention. They often lack awareness that their communication exclusively focuses on negatives and never on positives. The 4 Steps of Alignment mitigate this behavior by asking people to share compliments. During this step of the process, be sure to insist the curmudgeon share *something* they like.

Curmudgeonly behavior should be allowed. However, sometimes the curmudgeon can become toxic, expressing themselves in an edgy manner with huffs, rolling eyes, and crossed arms. If the curmudgeonly behavior crosses the line into crankiness, you must address it. Keep in mind that misery loves company and bad moods are more contagious than the flu. If you notice crankiness spreading, take a break. When you bring the group back into the room, it can be helpful to do a fun two-minute activity: play a video, tell a joke, or move around to lighten the mood.

During the break, check-in with the curmudgeon to make sure he is not holding back on an unvoiced concern. Let him know that you value his common sense and sensitivity to risk but are concerned about the edginess showing up. Frequently, the person is not in touch with a deeper concern, and your probing can help him express it more constructively.

9. FLIP-FLOPPERS

Flip-floppers are players who are hard to pin down. At one meeting, they see things one way; the next, another way. Instead of voicing their opinions openly, they tend to agree with whoever spoke last. Often flip-floppers are noncommittal, expressing themselves ambiguously. I can tell I'm dealing with a flip-flopper when they say they will do something but never say *when* they will do it. This evasive, peacemaking behavior is just accommodating reactivity. The person may only see the positive points in every argument. However, it's more likely that they fear they will displease someone and lose favor if their views don't match up.

If you have a flip-flopper in the group, it may be a sign that you haven't created enough psychological safety. A good strategy to prevent this behavior is to ask the flip-flopper to express their views first when asking for feedback. If the behavior persists, be sure to check in with the flip-flopper privately. It can be helpful to ask questions to help them shore up their views without being swayed by someone influential. It can also be helpful to challenge them to commit to and defend their own point of view.

10. PERFECTIONISTS

Perfectionists seek the perfect solution to every problem. They can help raise standards, but they can also bog the group down with overanalysis or excessive detail. One way to keep perfectionistic behaviors in check is to explicitly set a lower bar. Let people know that there are no bad ideas and no perfect solutions. Share the 80/20 rule. Using expressions like this can redirect perfectionists to seek practical solutions that are good enough to suit the need at hand.

TALK ABOUT IT

Keep in mind; we are all prone to use at least one of the unproductive strategies above to get our needs met. Normalize that these will come up from time to time and learn how to talk about them. Teambuilding activities can be helpful in cleaning up some of these patterns.

One teambuilding activity to consider is asking your team to pick the disruptive behavior they are most likely to fall into. Ask what might trigger that behavior in them what they would want their teammates to do to help them snap out of it. For example, I know that I tend to fall into grandstanding and narcissism. I love it when the team picks up my exact words and puts them in our final product. When this doesn't happen, I can harp on why my language is best. What can be helpful to me when this occurs is for teammates to acknowledge my idea was a good one but may not be best for the given moment. By acknowledging this pattern of behavior in myself with others, I not only become aware of my disruptive patterns, but I also grant permission for my teammates to intervene and get me back on the right track.

COACH, COACH, COACH, CHANGE

One last word about disruptors. Every once in a while, you might run into someone who is so incapable of cooperating that there is no turning them around. If you've tried at least three times to help the person, you may need to just accept the fact that there is nothing you can do.

While we like to think of humans as civilized and rational, in reality, we are much like wild animals. When you are leading groups, you are like a lion tamer who could get bitten. If you have someone who behaves in a manner that feels "off" or dangerous, look for ways to minimize their involvement. If you can, remove them from the group. It may be hurtful to the person, but don't feel guilty because your allegiance should be to the company, the process, and the group, not to one person. Just don't blame yourself. Try your best, but you can only do so much.

The bottom line is this: if the above problematic behaviors go on too long, you may never reach true alignment. Keep in mind this rule of thumb: Coach, coach, coach, change. What this rule means is if the person doesn't shift out of the disruptive behavior after being coached three times, they will probably never change. At that point, you need to change something by managing the disruptor out of the group.

CHAPTER 21

MAYBE YOU ARE THE TROUBLE

"Don't accept your dog's admiration as conclusive evidence that you are wonderful."

—ANN LANDERS

My client Eva was on a team of pro bono consultants working on charity cases. Eva was super passionate about the work and wanted to make sure the team represented their clients well. Unfortunately, with volunteers coming in and out of the project, details got missed, and balls were dropped. Eva became very frustrated and proactively brought up ideas for case improvement, but her teammates started to avoid her and reject everything she proposed. Why?

As I worked with Eva, we discovered that her high standards just were not realistic. Part-time volunteers could not be expected to know or follow exacting procedures. Furthermore, she was exhausted from picking up all the pieces and struggled to manage her reactivity. As you can imagine, her edginess made her message hard to hear.

If your story is like Eva's and you feel you are continually facing resistance, guess what? Your problems share a common denominator: you. Start by looking in the mirror. Ask yourself: Am I creating the problem? Whether you are or not, if you change what you are doing, you might discover a breakthrough.

If you are visionary, you likely arrive at ideas well before those around you. This is good news as it puts you in a position to lead others to new possibilities. However, it's not unusual for disillusionment to creep in if the gap between the way things are and the way you wish they were is too wide. You may wonder why people are so blind and don't see things the way you do. After all, isn't the challenge or solution just as plain as the nose on their face? Actually, probably not.

It's not unusual for an idea that is ten-out-of-ten important to you to be two-out-of-ten important to those you are trying to lead. This is not because your ideas don't matter. It's just human nature for people to be lost in their own world and lose sight of the bigger picture. You may be underestimating how much you know that others don't. Keep in mind, if you get too far out ahead of those you are leading, they will not be able to see you, and you will lose your chance to reach alignment.

Here is the bottom line: *start where they are,* not where you wish they were. Accept the reality you are in, knowing change is always possible. Perhaps those around you need some education, or maybe they are just too preoccupied at the moment to give you their full attention. Take a few deep breaths, take a walk, and reflect on what you can do to help them catch up. Whatever it takes, manage your reactivity, fears, and energy. Shapeshift them into creative energy. Stop talking about problems and what is not happening. Start talking about possible options for moving forward to create the outcomes you desire.

If you move faster than those you are leading, sometimes you have to slow down and have patience so they can catch up. Be careful not to complain when people "just don't get it" or make snide comments about others' beliefs. Even if you are more diplomatic than that, be careful not to let your negative energy spill out in subtle ways such as an edgy tone, rolling eyes, or pulling away. You may think people don't notice, but they do, and your negative energy will make them run from you.

If you are hitting a wall, don't blame the wall; blame yourself. Notice how you are showing up. If you find yourself always talking about the problem, then you are in reactivity, and your energy is undermining the likelihood of alignment.

TOP 10 BEHAVIORS YOU NEED TO MANAGE

Here are the ten most common reactive behaviors you might need to manage:

1. YOU ARE TOO ATTACHED TO YOUR IDEA

If you are a passionate advocate for your idea, you are blocking co-creation. People will feel overwhelmed or that you are not listening. Lower your intensity and passion. Double down on inquiry. Slow things down to explore others' points of view without refuting them. When someone offers a contrary point of view, be sure to validate the grain of truth in what they are saying. The more open you are to their ideas, the more open they'll be to yours.

2. YOU MAKE INTUITIVE LEAPS THAT OTHERS CAN'T FOLLOW

Try to remember what you didn't know when you first heard about the topic at hand. Build a map of your ideas by breaking them down into smaller steps and adding in the missing information. If necessary, write up talking points to provide a quick education to people less familiar than you with your proposed solution.

3. YOU PLAY DEVIL'S ADVOCATE TOO MUCH

If you have been challenging others' ideas, don't be surprised if they try to sink your next one. Instead of engaging in this vicious cycle, look for opportunities to support other's ideas. Double down on commending others' views publicly. If you do this often, you will build enough goodwill that others feel inclined to support you.

4. YOU THINK EVERYONE ELSE IS A BLEEPING IDIOT!

If you find yourself infuriated by how ignorant/incompetent/lazy/selfish everyone else is, then you are the problem. Trust is a teeter-totter. If you want people to trust and respect you, you have to trust and respect them. Your distrust of others is setting *you* up not to be trusted. Whether you express your disapproval aloud or not, people will sense your negative feelings about them and will send that energy right back to you. You may not realize it, but your ego is making you act superior to those you are trying to lead. Even if you are a genius, this doesn't mean everyone else is clueless. You can never align people you disrespect. To turn this around, look for the good in others and give them the benefit of the doubt. Find the most generous interpretation of their actions possible and lean into the possibilities that your positive regard will bring.

5. YOUR IDEAS ARE JUST TOO REVOLUTIONARY

It is essential to realize that culture will eat strategy for lunch. If you are working in a conservative culture, don't be surprised when your colleagues don't like your newfangled ideas. Maybe it is time to ask yourself if you are in the right environment. You may be a diamond in the wrong setting. Sometimes it helps just to move on and find a home for your ideas elsewhere.

6. YOU RUSH THINGS

Rushing is a pervasive issue. It's common to underestimate the time required to explore a new idea. If you are trying to cram a two-hour discussion into a half-hour agenda slot, you are bound to fail. Don't settle for less time than you need. However much time you think you need, ask for double. If you finish early, no one will complain.

7. YOU ARE TRYING TO MOVE FORWARD SOMETHING YOU DON'T BELIEVE IN

Faking endorsement never works. If you don't believe in what you are saying, no one else will either. Work to resolve your own misgivings about the challenge and solution you are moving forward or ask to recuse yourself from the task if you can. Always be honest and transparent about your own beliefs. If you don't, you will lose others' trust, and achieving alignment will get harder.

8. YOU PUSH FORWARD WHEN PEOPLE AREN'T READY TO LISTEN

If you are bringing forward an item for consideration, make sure your listeners are in the right headspace to hear it. Don't just rush in and start spouting off an idea. Instead, ask if they have time to hear you out. This request could sound like: "I've got an idea I'd like to run by you. I think it will take about thirty minutes. When might you have time for that?"

9. YOU MAKE OTHERS WRONG

If you position your proposed solution as a fix for a mess someone made, then you are just setting yourself up for a fight with the mess makers. Have some respect for the work that happened before you came along. Give credit for previous efforts. Always position your ideas as an evolution of the good work that precedes it, not a fix.

10. YOU GET STUCK IN EITHER/OR THINKING

If you are in a tug-of-war of opposing views, the conversation can become polarized. For example, your argument for why a system needs to change may trigger arguments for the merits of sticking with the system. In reality, you need to consider both the benefits of sticking with the system and the benefits of replacing it. To break the log jam, switch from either/or to both/and thinking. Leaders who manage polarities well face fewer power struggles and can steer groups toward more balanced and robust solutions. To learn more about how to manage polarities, I recommend reading *Polarity Management: Identifying and Managing Unsolvable Problems* by Barry Johnson. The theories in this book are life-changing.

The top ten list above is by no means comprehensive. The only way to honestly examine how you may be in the way of alignment is to ask others for feedback. Regularly ask how your leadership is impacting alignment and listen with an open mind. It can also be helpful to work with a coach who can provide an objective point of view and help you strategize ways to get yourself and others into a less reactive, more creative frame of mind.

IF NOTHING IS WORKING, LET GO GRACEFULLY

If it feels like you are getting nowhere, it may be time to ask yourself, *"Is this the battlefield I want to die on?"* Remember that you can always pick up the fight later when conditions or players change. The best ideas tend to have a life of their own; ideas will resurface if they are truly worthwhile.

If your ideas have been squashed by naysayers, take the high road. Let go of any resentments you may be holding on to. You only poison the waters of your future ideas by complaining that those who didn't back up your ideas are incompetent, clueless, or lack integrity. People value their reputation above all else, and if they find out that you have been bad-mouthing them, you may create enemies for life. You may think that what is said in private won't get out, but it always does! It's fine to fight the good fight, but once it is over, be sure to bury the hatchet because you never know when that relationship might be instrumental to your future.

Never take things personally; if you do, you can fall into victim thinking. People will pick up on that energy and pity you or see you as an immature whiner. If you do have an adversary in your way, play the long game by shifting focus to what you have control of and perform well there. With any luck, you will outlast your nemesis.

It is wise to cycle back around to all players, especially those who disagreed with your point of view, to offer SHUVA and reset your relationship going forward. By letting go and moving on with grace, you empower yourself and conserve your energy for future efforts.

SECTION 7. MEMORABLE SUCCESS FORMULAS

- Never, ever let anyone lose face in public
- Fear is inversely proportional to innovation

- Coach, coach, coach, change
- If you get too far out in front, they won't be able to see you
- Your problems all have the same common denominator: you
- If nothing is working, let go gracefully

Made in the USA
Las Vegas, NV
23 October 2024